Off

A Sports

David Rushworth Smith

Foreword by John Motson

Marshalls

Other published titles by the same author:

The Final Return of the Lord Jesus
Sickness in Christians
Christian Extremism
Christ Manifested
Altogether Lovely
Lies and Slander
Divine Healing
Living Stones
John Fletcher
Fasting

Dedicated to the lads and staff of the Tottenham Hotspur Football Club, who taught me all that I know and who bore my mistakes so graciously.

Marshalls Paperbacks
Marshall Morgan & Scott
3 Beggarwood Lane, Basingstoke, Hants, RG23 7LP, UK

First published by Marshall Pickering Ltd.

British Library CIP data

Smith, David R.
Off the ball: a sports chaplain at work.
1. Tottenham Hotspur Football Club—Chaplains
I. Title
796.334'63'0942188 GV943.6.T6

ISBN 0-551-01194-7

Phototypeset by Brian Robinson, North Marston, Bucks.
Printed in Great Britain by
Hunt Barnard Printing Ltd., Aylesbury, Bucks.

Contents

Foreword

The most arresting quality of this book is that its author believes he failed. If that sounds a contradictory recommendation, then bear the thought in mind as you read on.

The sheer dilemma facing the sports chaplain at work—and it is one with which any priest or clergyman would readily and sympathetically identify—is that the harder he tries and the more unswerving his dedication, the less he seems to have achieved and the greater the test of his faith.

In other words, the task is so boundless that any sense of progress is immediately dwarfed by the mountainous realization of what remains to be done. Any token achievement, be it a problem solved or a strain softened, can only be said to be scratching the surface, such is the stress and gathering confusion which professional people have thrust upon them, or impose upon themselves. In sport, peculiarly so.

It was into this challenging area that David Rushworth Smith chose to go as part of his ministry. The first thing the reader should know is that there was no question of his doing the sports chaplain's job full-time. While maintaining the total responsibility for his church and pastoral work in the community, this modest and unassuming parson offered the rest of his time to Tottenham Hotspur Football Club. He will not thank me for revealing that his health and his family suffered.

But the personal and professional sacrifices he made are of no moment here, and to dwell upon them would embarrass the author and detract from the impact of his book. Let us be content with saying that a full-time chaplain could scarcely have done more.

From my own privileged position as a television reporter covering Spurs' affairs in those years, I was struck not so much by the chaplain's presence – we had met through the 'Christians in Sport' organization and he was always discreet in his dealings with the players – but by his selfless industry.

If Tottenham were playing away in the north of England, he would be there with them on the coach if it was humanly possible, and occasionally when it was not. He was shamelessly prepared to make up for two days of his normal work lost, by overloading himself in the five which remained in that week.

Even when his own ministry in North London made travelling with the football club out of the question, the chaplain's spirit of concern extended to his seeing the players off when they left the ground, and waiting in the darkness for their return.

Part of the attraction of the pages which follow, is his own account of how the players responded to him. Many of them appreciated his wisdom and guidance only after he had gone – others maybe not at all. He never preached at them, took care not to intrude, and his prayers were unsolicited often. But his slight, bustling figure, head cocked in fussy concern, would be at their side if needed, or over their shoulder when an unexpected crisis tested the maturity of young and vulnerable athletes.

If he ever felt rejected, he never let it show. And there, I think, lay the true value of David Rushworth Smith's short but eventful ministry in the enclosed, harsh world of First Division football. His was the concern of a caring Christian – not the Bible bashing of an insensitive evangelist.

What he and others like him have built is a platform from which regular spiritual advice could be available to professional sportsmen and sportswomen. It is a position which he knew would take time to establish, but under which early cynicism on the part of those the chaplain seeks to help can give way to a ready response.

How he approached this specialized field, and how he dealt with the problems which he met, we can read in the pages that follow. I found it absorbing, sometimes heart-warming, and occasionally quite disturbing.

But I am delighted to leave the reader to this book, knowing that it is the first of its kind. For that reason, among others, I am thrilled to be able to reassure its author that far from failing, he constructed, under the guise of his own profound modesty, a significant spiritual signpost to the future.

John Motson,
St Albans,
1984.

Introduction

The Tottenham Hotspur lads train at Cheshunt, several miles out from the White Hart Lane ground. One morning, as I arrived, it was easy to see that there was an unusual colour weaving its way between the others on the field. The odd man was quickly recognizable as John Gorman, the lively Scottish footballer.

John had been in the squad at the Spurs when I first joined them, but this day he was on vacation from a famous Florida team, and could not resist the temptation to do some training with the lads he had earlier played with.

At the end of the training session, John bounded over the field towards me, with arms outstretched, and gave me a fine demonstration of a North American bear hug. We had not met for two years, but it was impossible to miss the genuine warmth of his welcome. Walking back to the dressing room, he had his arm round my waist, as the conversation flowed on continuously.

Two things came into my mind, as we caught up with each other's news, and exchanged information about the state of soccer on both sides of the Atlantic.

First of all, I wondered if there were any spies from FIFA amongst the visitors, because the Secretary of this august body had recently issued instructions about players not embracing on the field. I did not want to be the first one to be reported in the columns of the *Sun* newspaper!

Secondly, it dawned upon me that I must have made some kind of impression upon one sports personality, if this was the reception that I might expect after a two years' absence. I suddenly realized that my hours of effort had not been in vain, and that my work as a soccer chaplain had been of some use.

My years at Tottenham are now well-known, because of the publicity about my role there. The articles that have been written in the newspapers and magazines of the world are too numerous to mention, but they all played their part in making the work of a sports chaplain that much more easy.

The outcome of all that published material, as well as my successful sports column in the *Christian Herald*, resulted in me being asked to write some sort of record of my experiences, and my views about the role of those who take up the task of chaplain.

I cannot presume that these pages are any kind of study book for every future budding chaplain, but I trust that they will be of some assistance to sports directors, coaches, managers, physiotherapists, sportspeople, players, and fans. It is time that the sports world woke up to the importance of the work of chaplains, and used them more fruitfully.

David Rushworth Smith 1984

The Baptist Church,
Westbury Avenue,
London N22.

1: Getting The Role Right

Just when everyone was settling down, either to watch a video film or take a well-earned rest on the homeward journey, Don McAlister came towards the back of the coach where I was sitting and chatting with Jock the chef. I had not yet been involved at Tottenham for a month, and the newness was obvious. We were on our way back after another long-distance away-match, and I was still feeling my feet, not knowing where to go, or where to be, at any one moment. So far, the lads had maintained a respectful distance, not quite sure what to make of this extra man on the staff. The introductions, and my weekly presence, had not answered all their queries. I was still very much a new boy.

Don slid into the coach seat beside me, obviously intending to talk about something important, or ask a pointed question. Don McAlister is instantly likeable, and has a straightforward Northern-English approach, without delicate etiquette. Already, I had taken a liking to him, and had some chats about cars and engines, which are his second love. I knew that he would not beat-about-the-bush, whatever the subject he intended to raise.

'Dave, just what is your role at Tottenham? Why are you with us?' It was a question which ought to have had, by that date, a good answer, but I was not yet ready to give it. Three years later, I was better able to give such an answer to all who asked, but at that time, still wet behind the ears, I was unable to say much.

It had been vague from the start. There had been no guidelines, and there was nobody in Britain who could supply me with any. The function of a sports chaplain had not been properly defined then, and even letters from experts in America did not help much. From the point of view of the players, it seemed as if a clergyman was now all too often present, whereas there had not been one before. This placed some restrictions on their behaviour, and they had every reason to wonder if such restrictions were beneficial.

In time, one can imagine that players may get used to the idea of a local pastor popping into their dressing-rooms, and having long chats, but Don had not met it before, and he was rightly confused. He wanted to know if I was paid, what I hoped to achieve, and what the lads would get out of it. Knowing that he would tell the rest, I took my opportunity and expressed myself as well as I could. When I undertook to do this work, I could see that it would not be easy for me, because I was treading on new ground, and seeking to establish something that was rare in my country. I was glad that it had been Don who undertook to approach me, on behalf of the rest. I could imagine the anxiety if someone with less understanding had been sent to those back seats!

A help or a hindrance?

When I started at Tottenham, the club was in the Second Division, and working hard to get back into the First. One of those who was brought in to help the team back into the top ten, and on to the Wembley trail, was Osvaldo Ardiles. He had been bought from an Argentinian club in order to introduce a new style of play, and raise standards. This was a fortunate step both for the club and for myself, because if anyone understood my role and ministry, it was Ossie. He grasped the purpose of my time with the players, without having it explained, because of his background and upbringing. In the years after he joined us, he was to play an important part in making me acceptable. His professionalism and his understanding helped me again and again.

When Ossie arrived, I recognized that he would be a big help to me, and so I tried to encourage a friendship with him. That proved very difficult because his knowledge of English was not good in the early days, and my Spanish was poor. However, that was a small problem for someone who was reaching out for straws to clutch, in order to build something worthwhile.

A football club is made up of all kinds of people. I grew to appreciate them all, but realized that there were immense differences between them. Those differences did not make my task any easier, as I sought to have a role amongst them. Those who had been fortunate enough to have a university training were instantly approachable. Their college days had turned them into chatty people, who understood professional roles and grasped motives quickly. They had no problem in recognizing what I could do and why the club had opened its doors to me.

Unfortunately, this was not true of them all, and even those who had been in Sunday Schools, or who had attended churches, did not see my presence as a desirable thing. What was true of the lads was equally true of the ground and office staff. Some could not grasp why a clergyman should be allowed behind the scenes in a football club. For them, sport was sport and religion was religion, and there was an impenetrable barrier between them. Some deliberately used only four-letter words in my presence, in order to educate me along those lines.

When it was discovered, very slowly, that I had been an engineer before I had been a pastor, and when it dawned upon the most obstinate that I could be more outspoken than themselves, the opposition began to disappear. By talking about my earthy factory years, and by firmly standing up to all those who tried to brow-beat me, respect began to grow in those who openly opposed me at the beginning. In fact, at the end, my best friends were those who had deliberately tried to keep me out when I started!

Creating a role

If the reader has ever had to create a new job, where one did not exist before, he or she will recognize the problem that faced me. Not only was I supposed to do it, but I had to decide what it was that I was supposed to do, and please everyone, as I did it. The task was enormous.

I began by trying to create an identity for myself that had some association with the work of pastors in other areas of life. I was helped in this by the chef who accompanied the squad in their touring coach when they went off on long journeys. He had been in the armed forces, and so he was used to there being officers *and a padre*. In fact, during the whole of the time that he was with the Spurs, in that role,

Jock (as we all affectionately knew him) never called me anything but 'Padre' in all conversations.

The difficulty in my attempt to portray myself as a kind of sports 'padre' was that hardly anybody on the staff had been in the armed forces, and so they had never met either the word or the kind of person who fulfilled that role. Apart from Johnny Wallis, and a few on the security staff, a *padre* was no more meaningful than a *chaplain*. To them, both words were foreign.

I next tried to convey the sort of work that chaplains do in other spheres. Surely, they had all heard of chaplains in hospitals? Well, yes, they had, but they identified those people with situations in which somebody was *dying*. Did not a chaplain appear in hospital, at a bedside, when the doctors had decided that there was no more hope? After a little explanation, Pat Welton (who was then the assistant manager) grasped this picture perfectly, and we became completely adjusted to each other on this basis. However, for the lads who had not been in hospital, and had not had the opportunity of meeting a hospital chaplain, this notion was unreal.

It became obvious that a role had to be created by doing the job, and by doing it for long enough to make a picture come to life in people's minds. Then, I hoped the lads would not ask me what my role was; they would have become used to it. That was the plan, and the manager approved of this approach. In fact, he encouraged me to realize that it would take time, by saying that we need not expect to see much progress inside a year, and he was right!

Having a plan is one thing, but making it come to life is quite another, and especially if nobody else knows what the details are. Since such details were being worked out as we went along, everybody was in the dark from the very beginning.

The experts in America had written and told me that it was imperative that I was myself a soccer player from the past. This was going to prove difficult because I had played rugby football when young, and had not risen to giddy heights even there! Also, they had written to say that I must start where I intended to finish, and so begin by insisting on prayer with the team before each match. I decided to ignore both aspects of their kind advice and 'do my own thing'. At my age, I could not pretend to be an expert in soccer, because any sudden question would floor me. Also, in the situation in which I found myself, prayer before a game would not have been well received.

If someone is given a job to do, he must first prove to everyone that there is a job that needs doing, and that he has the ability to perform the task which everyone now sees is required.

What can a chaplain do, in a sports club, that others have not done, or cannot do? Answer that question, and we know what the role of a chaplain is. To help me, I enlisted the assistance of someone who was on the staff already, and who knew the profession like the back of his hand. This was Harry Hughes, a one-time Chelsea star and now the manager of the Spurs shops. Harry was one of the fully committed Christians on the staff then, and his advice proved invaluable. In the first few months, I spent hours of his spare time, asking questions about the way in which footballers think, spend their leisure hours, approach a game, view their manager, and a hundred other matters. He was very patient and forbearing with someone who had to learn everything from scratch. Better than that, Harry gave me the kind of encouragement which I needed in those early days, when I made so many mistakes.

How much time each week?

It soon became obvious that a chaplain could give five full days a week to the squad and staff of a First Division club, and then not do everything properly. The scope grew as I understood the situation better.

At first, I thought that I would be helping only the actual footballers. Very quickly, I found that I was being approached by all kinds of members of the staff, including the part-time Saturday staff. Within a few months, the fans began to realize that I was on call and they felt that I was there for them also! My contacts grew from a handful into thousands within two years.

A chaplain is a kind of neutral person. He belongs, and yet he is not an ordinary member of the staff. In a hospital, a patient can talk to the chaplain and know that the conversation will be confidential; it is quite different from talking to a nurse, a doctor, a cleaner, or a member of one's family. The whole relationship is on a different level. This is just how things developed for me. I could be approached by anyone in need of advice, and although I was apparently one of the officers (and in close contact with the directors), everyone knew that no gossip would develop from things shared.

At the beginning, I did not refuse any chat, approach, or request, because I was anxious to make headway and make friends as quickly as possible. I don't think that I was wrong to follow this course, but I soon found that my own church work was suffering from lack of attention. That had to be taken into account in due course, because I seemed to be spending more time 'in football' than 'in the parish'. However, by doing this, I made myself available to everyone, and quickly became known.

From the beginning, I knew that it would be of no value asking the players themselves what they wanted from my work at the club. I knew that young lads do not appreciate what anyone else does, until they have experienced it themselves. Youthful ideas do not often contain wisdom. For that reason, I did not ask the lads if they would tell me what I might do for them. Instead, I explained to each one, in turn, what my role was, and where I could help, if necessary. This took time, but it proved invaluable.

Slowly, my involvement grew, taking up more and more time each week. At first, I appeared only as they ended their last training session of the week, and spoke to as many as possible, as they prepared to go home (if it was a local match the next day), or as they climbed on to the coach which would take them off for the weekend to an away-match. After they had got used to seeing me around, then I began to appear at the final training session, even being on the field, or in the gymnasium, with them. When they had accepted me in that situation, then I began to appear both before and after each game, talking to them as they went into the dressing room, and as they emerged. When I found that there was no reaction to these further appearances, then I began to attend the training sessions on a Monday morning as well, and to make irregular appearances in the changing-room and showers. In order not to upset anyone, or create any disturbances, I made these changes slowly, over a long period of time, so carefully did I add to the duties. However, at the end of two years, I had created a role – I was a part of the scene.

The sports writers

The people who did not fully understand either who I was, or what I was supposed to do, were those who should have grasped it the most quickly – the journalists. These gave me a hard time, in all sorts of ways, until I impressed upon them that I was in *their* game and that they should treat me more kindly. My union card as a writer was flashed under their noses more than once, in an attempt to befriend them and win their support. It is clear that there are still some sports writers who cannot grasp what sort of a role a chaplain can have in a football club, and it is possible that they never will.

Because the work I have been doing had not been adequately defined before, there was nothing that I could refer to, and nothing I could refer others to, either. That was a considerable barrier, in the beginning, but things ought to be easier for other chaplains now, because more and more people in sport are grasping the role that such a person plays in a club, or profession.

Since more and more pastors are taking up this work, the situation will improve, and that can only be good news for those sports in which chaplains are given an opportunity.

A kind of definition

So, what is a sports chaplain, and what does he do? If I had been asked to write down answers to these questions two years ago, I would have dashed off several paragraphs easily. Now, I find it much more difficult. This is because my understanding of the task has widened. My conversations with sports personalities in other countries have shown me that this is a huge ministry if applied to all sports on all continents. Because of my wider view today, my definition is not short or simple, but I will try to limit it to one sentence.

A sports chaplain is a trained pastor who gives much of his time to the spiritual and emotional care of sports people and those who assist them in the furtherance of sporting activities, both amateur and professional.

2: Drugs, Gambling And Alcohol

I was in New York, in the summer of 1983, when the news broke that one half of all American football players were using drugs regularly. The reaction was total! Every newspaper carried the story, and every TV and radio station relayed the most up-to-date facts then being discovered about this overwhelming information. The *New York Daily News* carried a five-part series on the subject, after careful research by Brian Burwell, and nothing could have broken into the balm of the heat of that summer like this story.

The reporter claimed that there were approximately 10 players in every American National Football League team using cocaine on a regular basis. This seemed to be shocking until we all realized that he was speaking about *averages*. Brian Burwell went to a lot of trouble to make sure that every reader understood that he did not mean that *all* the teams had *half* of their players on drugs, but that 50% of *all players* were involved, and that only two teams did not have a problem. The revelation that one famous team had been investigated by the NFL, who had discovered that 34 players there were into cocaine was a blow, and the NFL Commissioner, Peter Rozelle, had to confess publicly that Burwell had 'done his research well'. By the time that I reached Cleveland, this information was making the headlines on newspapers from coast to coast, and causing comment at every level. The cab drivers opened up a conversation on this topic, instead of on the high humidity (which was on everyone's minds just then). Even serious international news was pushed into second place, as TV newscasters informed everyone about the 'latest on the drugs story'.

International drug-taking

Hot on the heels of that North American news scare came the 1983 Pan American Games drug scandal. It seemed to be a summer of sensational drug stories for the poor weather-beaten USA. Sixteen athletes were officially disqualified from the 9th Pan-Am Games, so casting doubts on sport in Argentina, Chile, Nicaragua, Canada, Puerto Rico, Venezuela, Cuba, Colombia, the Dominican Republic, and the United States. As if this was not shocking enough, 12 American athletes flew out of Caracas for home, rather than be tested for possible drug use. It did seem as if many of those taking part were involved in the regular use of drugs.

Craig Neff wrote a long article for the influential *Sport Illustrated* in order to explain things to a worried nation. Without clarification, the attendance at sports events would suffer, and the Olympics would never be the same again. Certainly, if the Moscow-based *Sovietsky Sport* is to be believed, the majority of all American sports personalities must be on drugs, for their writers assumed that what applied to a few was true for all! However, as Craig Neff was anxious to explain, the testing equipment used at Caracas seemed to be far more sensitive than any other similar spectrometers and gas chromatographs the competitors had met before. If these machines could detect drugs taken as long ago as six months previously, they might assume that influenza medicine (long-since forgotten by the athlete) was proof of the use of banned drugs. Was the Caracas affair a planned way of creating fear in the minds of all athletes, in every country, in order to ensure that the 1984 international Olympic Games would be free from rumour and gossip? Certainly this is how many world sports writers have seen it, because the testing procedures at Caracas were later shown to have been no different from those at other international sporting events in previous years. Dr Manfred Donike of the College of Sports in Cologne, who provided the staff and equipment at Caracas, insisted that the methods and the machinery were identical. In other words, it is possible that the 9th Pan-Am Games were used, like some piece of propaganda, to instil fear into all athletes everywhere that 'we mean business' (as

William E. Simon, the President of the US Olympic Committee, put it).

Suddenly, it appeared that Peter Ueberroth of the Los Angeles Olympic Organizing Committee should not have said (only seven months previously) that 'the only real drug problem that we have in the USA is football players taking cocaine'. Also, it appeared that the *New York Daily News* would have to widen its research, and include the hurdlers, the shot-putters, the long-jumpers, and all the other sports-people (including the swimmers, the golfers, and the tennis players), if their drugs survey was going to have any lasting influence on sport. The football players could not be the only ones stigmatized.

The moral dilemma

The Sports Section of the influential *Toronto Star* took the situation into the realms of reality when it dared to announce that there is no easy solution to this problem. Anabolic steroids and testosterone have been available to sportspeople since 1960, and have been used widely. By 1976 (when the Olympic Games took place in Montreal), it could be stated confidently that one half of all those taking part had used these drugs in some measure, at some time. Six competitors were disqualified then, but it was generally agreed that many more had deliberately stopped taking such drugs two months before the tests, so that urine samples would reveal nothing. As the *Toronto Star* said in August 1983, and as others have said since, this is an international moral dilemma, in a world where every nation wants to get a gold medal for something.

Dr Keith Walker of Edmonton in Canada is on record as having said: 'We have to decide ultimately what international competition is all about. If it is armed conflict, but using athletes instead of soldiers, then we are wasting our time using drug tests, because everybody is going to find a way round the tests and will continue to use drugs'. Dr Allan Ryan, member of the International Foundation of Sports Medicine, and one-time chairman of the American Medical Association's committee on sporting medicine, put the same idea in another way: 'If a child is told that it cannot do something, it assumes that there would be a lot of fun in doing it. In the same way, an athlete will use drugs if he knows that Olympic competitors are tested, because this tells him that drugs make a difference to an athlete.'

Clearly, anabolic steroids and testosterone will remain as possible helps for sportspeople in the same way that glucose used to be fifty years ago, until it is agreed internationally that they are dangerous to one's ultimate health and so are banned everywhere. That day may be years away, in view of the deep national longings in some countries for a gold medal at *any price*. Also, in view of the ability of some doctors – in some countries – to trick the most efficient testing equipment, we may never know the whole truth.

In his *Complete Book of Sports Medicine*, the eminent Dr Richard H. Dominguez wrote that *amphetamines* may appear to enable sportspeople to improve their performance temporarily, but any user can become addicted, and any addict can suffer brain damage. In the same vein, he wrote that *steroids* do appear to improve one's performance for competitions, but that there are serious long-term after-effects following prolonged use, including pituitary gland suppression, increased facial hair on females, greater risk of heart attack, greater risk of cancer, higher blood pressure, and personality irritability. Clearly, there is a moral dilemma for those who want to win (or improve their performance), and who know that the other man is using drugs in order to obtain the reward.

Whilst I was in Canada in 1983, *Sport Canada* issued a statement that they were prepared to fund and see that Canada, as a nation, developed a leadership role internationally, in order to ensure that every country tightened its internal controls over sportspeople and drugs, so that international competitions became simply competition between people, and not over who has been taking what.

Footballers and alcohol

In the 1960s I tried hard to get a letter published in the most renowned of the British daily newspapers on the subject of alcohol abuse. My letters were always returned with an apology. I wrote another (which I had carefully put together) and sent it with a personal letter to the editor saying that I would continue to write such letters until he finally published one of them, in view of the terrible harm being done to the health of so many by alcohol abuse. He kindly replied with a personal letter in which he said that there was no hope of his newspaper publishing such a letter because it would affect the advertising revenue too much. He had discovered, as many more have done, that commercial pressures can be very influential!

In my time at the Spurs, I never had to talk about drugs to any of the players or staff. I did spend a lot of time trying to help some of the supporters of the club who had become involved with drugs, but no one else. However, tobacco and alcohol presented some problems.

It is strange being telephoned and asked if drugs are a problem amongst the players 'at your football club'. It is like being asked to reveal secrets that you have been sworn to keep. It is a joy to give the honest answer and reply with a firm 'No', even though the American coach questioner finds it hard to believe. The newspaper reporters in America think that the British are lying if they make that reply, and don't print your answer, because their readers would not believe it anyway. I was never asked if tobacco and alcohol had been a problem, and so I did not have to reveal secrets.

For those of us who have studied medical evidence, tobacco smoke in a crowded room seems to be as harmful to the non-smoker as to the person smoking. Having that kind of knowledge makes different people of us. This was why I got a 'protection complex' about the football lads I cared about, if they were ushered into a smoke-filled room after a match. Those smoking did not seem to realize the harm that they might be causing to these valuable players. In fact, on one or two occasions, it seemed that a man could be a director of a football club and yet have no personal interest in the health and well-being of the very people who make that club successful. I had a similar impression about some of the office and ground staff. The players all seemed to be very sensible about the effects of tobacco. For that reason, I always preferred to use the Players Room before and after matches, rather than any other, because there smoking was very limited.

Alcohol abuse

In the film *Those Glory, Glory Days* (which is about the Tottenham Hotspur Football Club in 1961), Julie Welch did not say anything about the drinking habits of the lads. Considering that the team was seen in this film through the rose-tinted spectacles of a teenaged schoolgirl, this is to be expected. It took Jimmy Greaves to provide us with the 'behind-the-scenes' view of what it was really like, in his book *This One's On Me.* There, he tells us about men like Dave Mackay, Cliff Jones, Bobbie Smith, Bill Brown and John White, drinking quantities of beer in local public houses after the training sessions and matches. In fact, Jimmy openly admits in this revealing book, that it was at Tottenham where 'knocking back booze' became more than just a habit. After each successful game, the group of drinkers felt that 'a good long drink' was a fair reward for all their effort.

In my experience, a sportsman who does not drink alcohol is a very rare person. What is true of the darts champion is true of the golfer (and his proverbial 19th hole). It is a rare footballer who is on the teetotal wagon. However, I never had to deal with anyone who had the problem that Jimmy Greaves and others had to face when it was no longer a case of 'sport comes first', but 'I must have a drink first'. As we shall see in the chapter about violence, I came face to face with the way in which alcohol affects the behaviour of sports spectators but not the players, during my time at Tottenham. I remember a director getting drunk after one special match win, but even that only happened once to a player in my time, and that was when he realized that his constant relegation to the Reserves meant that he was hardly ever likely to be in the First Team again.

I have often wished that I had been around when Jimmy and his mates were hiving off to the White Hart for a bout of serious drinking, because then I should have had the experience of trying to help a talented sportsman who was ruining his life through this consuming passion. However, it was not to be, for Jimmy Greaves was out of the game before I began at the Spurs, and their experience of that earlier period had taught them a lot about heavy drinking and successful football.

When we recall what the misuse of alcohol did to Jimmy Greaves, and the way in which it reduced a remarkable champion First Division goal-scorer into an inmate of the alcohol unit of a mental hospital, it becomes obvious that alcoholism is not a joke. For this reason, despite the opportunities, I never did buy any of the Tottenham lads a drink and I warned most of them to remember Jimmy Greaves and Georgie Best when I saw them drinking.

The attraction of gambling

Even as I would consider it desirable for sports chaplains to be allowed to comment on the effects of drugs, alcohol and cigarette smoke on the health and vitality of sportspeople, so I would also consider it beneficial if they were allowed to speak on the subject of gambling. If there is a factor in life which really hurts the families of football supporters more than the cost of 'daddy travelling to away-matches', it is gambling. Unbelievable sums of money are spent each week by men and women who are unable to afford such amounts. Children, homes, family needs and health care are all ignored in the relentless search for riches through the fortunes of a team of lads whose efforts in any given week cannot ever be accurately forecast.

Soon after my arrival at Tottenham, I decided to assess the gambling attitudes of the players. In private chats with first this one, and then another, I discovered that the captain had given a firm lead to them all in refusing to be involved with any form of gambling on the outcome of matches, apart from a little private game on the away-match coaches. In all my years there, I did not hear of one player who filled in football coupons. A few of them backed horses, and they were almost all willing to take part in special charity 'draws' by buying tickets (and even whole books) from zealous charity workers, but nothing more than this.

Again, I have often wished that I had arrived earlier at the Spurs, so that I could have tried out some anti-gambling therapy on those who had been involved. Jimmy Greaves says that one of his mates placed bets on horses through the club telephones rather than an outside coin box. Then, having lost, he would borrow from the other lads to clear his betting debts. Gambling fever can be just as destructive as the pull of drugs, nicotine, and alcohol, and just as effective in ruining an up-and-coming sportsman.

I remember one Spurs fan who smoked heavily, drank far too much, and gambled away all the rest of his weekly income after he had paid to see the team play. He had no savings, his breathing was alarming, his mother was always in a state of distress, and his social life was confined to a tight-knit circle of public houses and football matches. When he was made redundant, his flow of cash decreased, and so his ability to gamble, buy tickets, and drink, was seriously curtailed. His whole fabric of life collapsed around his own ears, because he could not continue to support the mainstays of his own behaviour patterns. It was sad to see him walking down Tottenham High Road after that. He was a man without purpose, and without a reason for living. Despite efforts on my part, he refused all the kind of help that would have been a benefit. One wonders how many more there are like him?

The survivors

Jim Wilson had been the toast of Southend-on-Sea at one time, because he was one of those talented goal-keepers who could make it appear that the game would have been lost without him. Everybody in Essex knew Jim Wilson, and for a long time, he was the hero of every local schoolboy. That changed when alcohol became more important to him than anything else in life. His marriage suffered as well as his sport, and soon he became another derelict in London's East End.

Jim lives in quiet retirement in Westcliff now, and reflects on what might have been. Ray Clemence might have known a greater rival, but for the effect of drink on Jim. He could have worn an England cap, but for drink. However, although fame may be impossible now, and his health may never recover, Jim has found inner peace. His caring daughter took him along to a church in Leigh-on-Sea one night, and he suddenly realized that if the Lord Jesus did not help him, he was lost in this world and the next. Jim became one of the survivors. He even gave a few years to the London Embankment Mission, seeking to help the down and outs, who flock into that area when darkness falls.

Jimmy Greaves is another of the survivors. To see him as a confident presenter on television now, it is difficult to believe that he slipped so low in the 1970s. His present success is an encouragement to everyone who has a ministry to alcoholics in sport or elsewhere.

Unhealthy eating habits

Whilst I was at the Spurs, one of the lads was called the 'Billy Bunter of Football' in the newspapers, and another was declared to be a 'Junk Food Johnny'. One got into the habit of eating too much, whilst the other had for too long made a habit of eating the wrong food. This can be just as much a problem to a worried football manager as the other vices mentioned so far in this chapter.

During the years which followed the Second World War, eating habits amongst young people changed drastically and many became hooked on fast-food. This kind of fare may be excellent for a short time and sufficient in some occupations, but the hectic and demanding life of a sportsperson requires a proper and regulated diet. The lack of essential vitamins and minerals affects personal performance in due course.

The inexperienced young athlete is not aware of the old Chinese proverb that 'We are what we eat', and tends not to care. Only the experienced eye can detect the difference between the performance of those who have and those who have not been careful over their diet. An undisciplined young sportsman can be hopeless at understanding what the fuss is all about, and might easily find fault with anyone who seeks to lead him along more sensible dietary paths. Even demotion from the First Team might not achieve the result of getting a player to eat good food properly.

Do these things really matter?

The reader will doubtless have met the 95-year-old man who says that he owes his longevity to his daily vices, and who insists that his daily intake of alcohol, his 20 cigarettes per day, his gambling and indulgent eating, have done him good.

Sports chaplains have all met sportspeople who say something similar. As some frank autobiographies have revealed, sportsmen have taken to the field and track after being drunk the night before, or after slipping out of some girl's bed. It is on record that such lads have then gone on to do splendidly before the crowds of spectators. Does this mean that careful eating, teetotalism and non-smoking have no value in sport?

Statistics can be very annoying to those who are seeking the best for people. For this reason, the challenge of the 95-year-old playboy's testimony is not easy to handle. It appears to undo all the good that years of hard work have achieved.

However, such isolated testimony about vices have never convinced the experts because they are not provable. The scientists have shown us that cigarette smoking endangers health; they have shown us that alcohol abuse endangers health; they have shown us that over-eating and improper-eating endangers health. They have faced us with proven facts which only the stubborn person will ignore.

Showing that a wise sportsman does better than an unwise one is not easy, because scientific proof cannot be obtained immediately, and yesterday's game may have suggested the opposite. However, time is important to this debate. The performance of Jimmy Greaves when he was at the height of his career is one thing, but his inability to maintain that performance is quite another. His own story tells us why he declined in the way that he did. Clearly, these things do affect us, even if we will not admit it, and even if we cannot obtain immediate proof.

The role of a chaplain here

I was fortunate in that there were no problems with drug addicts, alcoholics, gamblers, or over-sexed footballers whilst I was at Tottenham. I would have been glad of the opportunity to help, but the chance never came. We can put that down to good management at the time. How would I have handled them if there had been opportunity? I should have taken exactly the same action that I have taken with others who have had these problems outside of sport, because where vices are concerned people are the same in every profession.

However, in every case there would have been complete confidence, since it is vital that stories do not circulate and that a player's character is not spoilt by gossip. Too many excellent sportspeople have had their reputations impoverished by idle words. Chaplains must be amongst those who build up reputations; they must not be amongst those who destroy them.

3: The Peril Of Fame

On the day when Terry Gibson was called into the First Team at Tottenham, in order to replace an injured player, I made sure that I was in the right place to help him after the match. When a 17-year-old lad is made to face a small army of journalists and is asked a succession of difficult questions, it is an agonizing ordeal. To have been 'dropped on' at short notice was not easy; to have faced the defence of the opposing side was enough of a hurdle in one day; now he had to say sufficient things to make a dozen bold headlines the next day.

As soon as it became apparent that Terry might say something that he would regret later and so spoil the occasion, I moved in and snatched him away from the Press, making suitable apologies, and led him to the privacy of the Players Room. Every new recruit to a First Team from the less experienced (and more junior) teams has to face this ultimate test of meeting the sports reporters. Even the most trained university graduates find this to be a daunting experience. For those less well-trained, interviews are a sort of necessary evil. In one way, it is enjoyable to be surrounded by those who are wanting to know your opinion (the pride in us all is pleased at such attention). In another way, it would be better if one could just get on with the job, and not be bothered by these questions. After a time, one learns that the demands of the public for the instant views of all famous people is only one price of fame.

Peril of youth

In the not-too-far-distant past, the majority of sportspeople were of mature years. Then, we passed through a phase when – if they were not of mature years – they were university graduates. At the present, we seem to be allowing mere youngsters to 'take the field', in order to obtain a more exciting form of game. The older man in professional soccer is a rare creature today, and increasingly this pattern is spreading. The results are not too difficult to envisage, especially if we continue to allow sports writers full access to all players for 'instant' comments.

Also, the patterns are easy to discern if journalists are allowed to continue to invent stories and put all kinds of comments into the mouths of sportspeople they have not even met. The younger we are, the less able we are to cope with this kind of journalism. Even mature sportsmen have been known to experience trauma when they read the kind of things that some writers have quoted them as having said.

Peril of fame

When the late Kenneth Allsop and I were neighbours in Hertfordshire, he used to talk a lot about the Yorkshire Cricket Club players with whom he was acquainted. He had been to school with one of them, met a few more in TV interviews, and chatted with several more in various public houses. On this basis, he felt (quite understandably) that he had a close liaison with the whole team. When he discovered, almost accidentally, that the captain was my cousin, he stopped conversing on this subject! After that, there had to be other mutual topics. What had stopped the flow of words? Nothing but the peril of fame. Since we were both Yorkshiremen, the ultimate in sportsmanship had come between us. One has to be of Yorkshire blood to know what power the captain of the county cricket team has upon everyone! That kind of power, through position, comes to every lad who makes the grade into the First Team and every girl who plays on the Centre Court at Wimbledon.

Peril of too much cash

It was a shock to me that some ordinary businessmen are willing to pay quite large sums of money in order to share a meal and then play a game of golf with local sports stars. These fellows take a day off from work and hand over far more than I can hope to earn in a fortnight in order to be able to tell their neighbours, business acquaintances, and mates, that they had been chatting to Steve Perryman or Glenn Hoddle yesterday. It is not surprising that every new professional in the team soon learns how to play golf! Overnight, mere lads become able to command large sums of money through personal appearances of one kind or another. What had been impossible 20 years previously, now is both possible and easy. Fame quickly turns naïve boys (who really only play football because they love the game) into wealthy young men.

It would have been wonderful if I could have arranged for all of the players to take it in turns to go into local schools, youth clubs, sports centres, and handicapped children's homes each week, but the majority were too busy, and some had their private businesses. We must be careful not to find fault with sportspeople who take their opportunities when they are offered them, because top class sport is not possible for many for long. Also, we must not forget those dedicated sports personalities who give so many hours each week in charity work. When I was at Tottenham, some of the lads were very generous with their time, and did not mind travelling long distances in their leisure hours, if the cause was genuine. I was often asked if a charity was genuine, and my opinion was always considered to be final. They trusted me to know the local conmen and the dubious charities, in order that they might make suitable excuses and avoid wasting their efforts. However, in view of the magnetic attraction of sports stars today, it is a pity that someone cannot ensure that each player's contract includes the necessity to be involved with charitable work at a local level. The price of fame should include a measure of involvement, in order for there to be a balance. The activities of a few do-gooders should not be allowed to provide the total 'responsibility package' for the whole of sport, however helpful such work is.

Peril of power

When I climbed on to the Greek airliner at Heathrow en route for Rodhos, I knew that everything was booked and that nothing could go wrong. At Athens, there would be another Greek plane waiting to take me to Rodhos, and on the island itself, my hotel booking was doubly confirmed. I could sit back and relax during the flight, because everything was arranged. The first shock came at Athens airport, where I was told that I had been too slow in transferring from the first flight and so the second flight had left without me. No amount of debate was able to change the situation. I would now arrive on Rodhos eight hours late.

This was more than a delay for me, because such a long wait would mean that I would not be able to watch the Athens versus Rodhos soccer match that evening, in the New Town stadius. However, there is little that one can do in the face of blunt refusal, especially when many metres of open sea intervene!

Upon arrival at the hotel on the island, I was confronted by shock number two. My room (that had been confirmed in writing) was now not available. The manager blamed it on the agency in London, little realizing that everything had been arranged through the Greek airline and that *he* had given the written assurance. Again, no amount of argument made any difference. I had to accept a room that was far from presentable, despite the fact that I had paid in advance for a room that was perfect.

The next day, it all became clear. I had not been too late for that second flight from Athens; the airline had squeezed the Athens team on board, by commandeering my seat and as many other booked ones as they required! And that room I had reserved? There had been no mistake in London at all; the manager had given the Athens team the best rooms in the place and pushed me along with others into any available space. Fame had made its mark by giving first place to those who belonged to a crack national team. This is another peril of fame: if one is not careful, sportspeople are treated as if they were more than human, and mortals are given lesser privileges. For young people, this is a more dramatic change of role than when a nursery teacher becomes a princess. Many young sportspeople handle it less well than Princess Diana, and suffer emotionally as a result.

Peril of competition

In his excellent book *Competition*, Gary Warner tells us of another aspect of the peril of fame which does not dawn on sportsmen and sportswomen immediately. Since sport is, by its very nature, a competitive involvement, everyone who takes sport seriously, or enters it in order to obtain a living, is in competition with everyone else in that sport. In the case of soccer, I have seen talented international forwards like Alan Brazil, Steve Archibald, Mark Falco and Garth Crooks compete with each other in training in order to be the ones selected to play in the next big match. Despite the fact that they were in the same team, and being paid by the same club (which was being supported by the same fans), they were in competition with each other for five days out of each week.

Gary Warner explains in his book that although there are obvious benefits from all competition, there are hidden dangers. He suggests that one of these hidden dangers is violence, and shows that the competitive spirit runs through the whole of sport, from the player to the smallest supporter, climbing over the barriers of school, town, county, state, and nation. This is something which has been mentioned rarely when violence in the sports stadiums is considered. National sports ministers talk about prison and fines when a crowd goes out of control, but not about the spirit of competition. Perhaps the link is clear only to those who have been kept on the bench when they knew that they should have been on the field.

Peril of stress

Quite apart from the spirit of competition, every athlete and sportsperson knows about stress. Even the golfer (who is supposed to be relaxing and getting sufficient exercise while playing) is under considerable stress when it comes to the last few holes, and his reputation is at stake.

Behavioural scientists in several countries have taken a great interest in this subject for more years than most of us realize, and have come to some interesting conclusions. Dr Joseph A. Pursch of California (who has had many eminent international patients in his care) suggests that those athletes who find fame at an early age do not know what life is without it, and so are in special peril. He says that when such a child sports star reaches the age of 21, he suddenly realizes that he is earning more than all of his family put together, and begins to come under stress purely from a guilt-consciousness. This may not make a lot of sense to those of us who are not in that situation, but documented evidence seems clear.

When Tommy Warren, the Florida football star, was jailed in 1981 on a marijuana conviction, he said that those in his position had been psychologically conditioned to feel that they were above the law and so could commit petty crimes and be overlooked by society.

Another eminent scholar who has written extensively on the subject of stress and its effect upon behaviour is Dr Lawrence J. Hatterer, of Cornell University Medical College. He has suggested that success for a young sports star can mean a total radicalization of the personality, with resulting behaviour patterns that would not have been believed possible previously.

Dr Arnold R. Beisser (a clinical professor of psychiatry) asks us all to ponder the question: 'Is there life after successful sport?', in view of the sudden rise to fame for some, because 'when someone has had everything that life offers whilst still young, how can he or she hope to find anything else in life that is equal to it when the fame departs?'

Goodbye to humility

Mick Michels is a famous sports writer in Belgium, who travels widely in search of stories for the Flemish *Sport* magazine. In 1982, Mick Michels journeyed from Brussels to London in order to get a story about Osvaldo Ardiles, prior to the opening match of the 1982 World Series in Barcelona. Upon arrival at Cheshunt, at the agreed time, Mick found that the subject of his article had not yet arrived for the training session, and was not likely to do so for several hours, in view of a change in the timing. Faced with a long wait, Mick approached me and asked for advice. I offered to take him round to Ossie's home in Wormley if–over the telephone–Ossie agreed to this. After confirmation, we set off and were greeted by Ossie's welcoming wife, Sylvia. For me, this was just part of the job. I was helping one of the lads and one of my journalistic colleagues. I thought no more of it until the article was published. The opening five paragraphs were a comparison between the life-style of the club chaplain and one of its stars! Even the difference in the sizes of the cars (a small Allegro compared with a long 4-litre Jaguar) was stated. After those opening paragraphs, Mick then gave all his talent to a full assessment of Ossie and his expectations in the World Cup. However, as a careful journalist, he had noted the symptoms which can so easily accompany fame. Instead of humility, showmanship takes over. After the big car has been bought, the larger house is obtained, and then the swimming pool arrives. Too quickly, the lad who is ever willing to learn, turns into someone who has everything and can be taught little. Mick was not criticizing Ossie; he was making a point!

A father-figure

In all of these realms, when fame arrives too quickly, introducing its various perils, a youngster needs fatherly advice from someone. In sport, when the young star is most vulnerable, he or she is often far from home and cut off from the support of parents and older brothers and sisters. Glenn Hoddle has freely admitted his debt to his parents at this stage in his own autobiography, but he was fortunate in having his home so close to Tottenham. This is rare.

As we know, there are sports agents to help young people in these confusing years, but in the past that role was filled by the manager, coach, captain, or club secretary. As history shows, some sports clubs have provided a better background for some rising sports athletes than their parents could. The advice and wisdom in some sports clubs is so considerable that I have been full of admiration. Some staff are so caring about their apprentices that they could not be in better hands if they were in hospital.

However, although this is true in some places, in others there is no concern for the players other than that they are fit to play in the next game. Because of this, I see a need for sports chaplains now, more than ever before. Whilst these could only be full-time in the more prosperous clubs, one-day-a-week chaplains ought to be possible in most clubs today, and they would be worth their weight in gold. As a real father-figure, showing a true concern for the lasting welfare of each player, a sports chaplain can encourage virtues which will balance the effects of sudden fame, and help to produce sports stars who are a blessing to society, in every way.

4: Facing Relegation And Promotion

In August 1983, the manager of Watford Football Club said that he would like to stand all the sports agents against a wall and shoot the lot of them! Doubtless this was said in the heat of an angry moment, but the papers will not let managers forget such memorable quotations, and—in any case—Graham Taylor spoke for many when he exploded on this subject.

As soon as a young sportsman hits the headlines these days, an agent will not be too far away to help him make the most of his opportunities. What is true of sports lads today will be true of girls in sport tomorrow, and has been true of entertainment stars for many years. In the present environment, we cannot blame the young people for making the most of their passing fame, whatever managers say. The ogre which faces every sportsperson is relegation, despite the promotion of yesterday.

Youthful ambition

In every large sporting club, there is a constant flow of young hopefuls who see themselves as up-and-coming stars of tomorrow. With ambition and conceit as their driving power, they apply to managers for positions which they cannot hope to fill, and speak disparagingly of those who turn them away, suggesting jealousy (and not professional ability) stopped them from becoming all that they had prophesied concerning themselves. I have sat and talked to some of these at Tottenham. The majority have faulted the management there for not seeing the potential or recognizing star quality in advance. It is a rare lad who blames himself for not achieving the possible.

Knowing that he was good, and wanting to help both him and his family, I went out of my way to promote a young West Indian lad who had shone in local matches. By careful approaches, and dropping words in the right ears, the day came when this boy was asked to attend training sessions so that his abilities might be assessed. He did so well that he was taken into the youth team.

The reader will assume that the lad was grateful and so worked hard to fulfil not only his own ambitions but also my own efforts on his behalf. In fact, it was not like that. He arrived late for training sessions, stayed out late the night before important matches, and gave the impression that he was indispensable. When he was sacked (with everyone's full approval), he criticized the management for being racial and accused them of not wanting a West Indian to succeed. That was the last time I did anything to help a 'rising star', and I had no sympathy with those who behaved like him.

International pressures

I did have a lot of sympathy for Jack Grant, however, when he was relegated in quite a different way, as a result of international pressures. Jack was born in 1907 in Trinidad, of European parents. By the time that he was 23, Jack had graduated at Cambridge, played soccer for the university, captained the West Indies cricket team on a world tour and become engaged to the daughter of a high-ranking Chief Justice in Zimbabwe. The sporting career which followed was exemplary. He was fêted in country after country, and given high awards. Because of this, and because of his fine academic qualifications, Jack Grant was made the Principal of Adams College in Durban, South Africa. In 1949, and long before most of us had heard of the word 'apartheid', Jack clashed with apartheid leaders. There then followed seven years of inconceivable persecution and tension, resulting in Adams College being 'liquidated'. In order to be true to himself, and to his belief that all human beings are equal in the sight of God, Jack finally had to leave South Africa. He died in Cambridge in 1978, still cherishing his passion for international sport, but sad to see so much strife in sport.

A change of course

When Peter Taylor left the Spurs to join Leyton Orient, I could see a great professional at the crossroads of his career. So far, he had been rising upwards, and everything had gone well. I could see that there might be drastic changes soon.

Peter is a Rochford lad who quickly attracted the attention of Southend United. From there, Peter transferred to Crystal Palace where he shone so much that he was chosen both for the under-23 and full England teams. In September 1976, Peter came to Tottenham. He was a great success, and his professional approach to the game was a bonus. To see him dribble his way through the weaving players, and then shoot at the goal mouth with cannon-fire energy was a weekly thrill for thousands. I quickly learned to believe in his accuracy, when he deliberately just missed my head, again and again, in the concrete gymnasium at White Hart Lane!

When it became necessary for him to endure major surgery, Peter took it all in his stride. The directors paid for him to have the very best treatment in a famous London hospital, and he received excellent care. However, I saw him the day after the operation, and I perceived that changes were on their way. The conversation was all about sport and his hopes for the future, but even when he fully recovered, Peter would be one year older, and there were a dozen lively young lads waiting in the Reserves to snatch his place.

He had a long chat with me before he left, just as others have done both before and since. He knew that things would be different, and that the Spurs fans would no longer flock to his sports shop at Westcliff, but he bubbled with enthusiasm about the future. His career had changed course and he would not be asked to play for England again. Such knowledge must have a profound effect upon anybody. Some will be miserable to their wives, others will go out and get drunk. Peter had many experiences to draw upon, and he knew the obvious hazards of professional soccer, but to meet a crossroad in one's career is different from anything else. Apart from rising to the giddy heights of large club coaching, or management, one could be on a downward slope, and that can be a depressing thought for any sportsman with a family to care for.

Out of the game

Again and again, I have asked young players if they know what happened to such-and-such a sportsman from the past. If they have heard of him (which is rare), they will very likely not be able to tell of his present whereabouts unless he has become a manager or a TV personality. The stars of tomorrow do not know what happened to the stars of yesterday. This is a phenomenon which is common only to the world of sport. In other professions, they have a much more caring attitude. Why, even booksellers have retirement homes for elderly booksellers, and most unions have convalescent homes for their injured. Sport does not have quite the same approach.

In a world where famous rugby football players are forced to quit on doctors' orders through injuries, and equally famour cricket players are forced to retire early through failing eyesight, we are all tempted to be uncaring for the sports stars who have fallen from view. Henry Cooper seems to have made a good transfer from the boxing ring to his present work, and–judging by the last chat that I had with him–he has no 'hang ups' over advertising body lotion on television. In the same way, Fred Perry appears to be satisfied that his name has given fame to the factory producing sports-wear only a stone's throw from the Spurs' ground. For a few, life has been good since relegation; for some it has even improved! However, for most, it has not been easy.

When Harry Hughes proposed to an attractive model he had the advantage of being a famous Chelsea football player. Life seemed to be full of hope when Joyce accepted, but he could not remain in the First Division for ever, and he knew that each year drew the end nearer. All sport careers can be short-lived and most of them are. Compared with most, Harry did very well. After Chelsea there was Bournemouth and those splendid years when the 'Giant-Killers' romped home to many victories. And, there were those English youth team tours, during which Harry endeared himself to so many new players. But then, and so close to the end of his career, a leg fracture broke the pattern of success. What does a footballer do when fame deserts and an injury gives so much doubt? Like others, Harry decided to invest everything in a sports shop. It would have been a great success, if the council had not directed all the trade away from its premises, in one of those development schemes. Now, what does an old-time soccer hero do, when he cannot run and his savings are lost?

Harry was fortunate. He found a niche as the manager of the Tottenham Hotspur shops. The energies that he threw into beating the Spurs 1957 team, during the FA Cup rounds that year, he now throws into making his souvenir shop one of the best in the world. Though out of the game, Harry is still in football, and it is providing him with a living. He knows that he has much to be thankful for, because he could be like so many others who are not only out of the game, but are forgotten.

The smell of success

As a teenager, Steve Perryman (now with an international reputation) approached Bill Nicholson – then the famous manager of the Spurs – and asked for a rise in pay under a proposed new contract. Bill (who always exudes a fatherly influence) looked the youngster in the eye and said, 'How many people come into this ground to watch you play?' Steve knew then that he had no pulling power, as far as crowds were concerned. We now know that he not only earned every penny that he was paid then, but that he was being underpaid before that particular contract was renewed. Success has a special ability to add to our natural sporting characteristics, and Steve Perryman discovered this.

On the other hand, Terry Naylor never seemed to have the success that he deserved, and this was bound to affect his play. I remember how sad he was at the turn-out for his testimonial game in the 1979–80 season, after all the promotional build-up. After giving unstinted effort, each sportsman expects a proper reward. One would have expected a greater response for Terry, in view of the apparent favour that the fans had for him. Despite his commitment, Terry realized that success did not necessarily accompany him at Tottenham, and so he soon moved to another club.

Why should success be such a fickle companion for those who seemingly deserve it? And why should one be successful and another not, when they both give just as much of their time and strength for the same cause? The questions are easy to ask, but difficult to answer. However, there is no doubt that success means everything where relegation and promotion are concerned.

Relegated to more fame

When Pat Jennings was told by the Spurs manager that he was extra to requirements, he felt as if his world had collapsed about his ears. This talented Irishman had come to Tottenham as a budding champion goalkeeper and had displayed remarkable abilities to save his team from defeat, even when his own defence had not been completely helpful. Pat is a quiet-spoken fellow, who gives the impression that he would not harm a fly, but when his big hands reach out for a soccer ball, he comes alive! For him, football is everything.

Pat was not the only one who was surprised by the news that Tottenham no longer wanted him. To part with Pat seemed like an attempt to destroy a vital asset, just when we needed every able hand. The supporters were horrified and angry. Pat was stunned, just as everyone who is declared redundant. In the providence of God, as he later pertly put it, Pat was invited to join the squad at Arsenal, where he has proved that he is a lasting star. This did not mean that Pat could only fulfil his true potential by moving to another club, because – as we all know – Pat was already at the height of his career when he left Tottenham. His record then (as we know from his own book and the statistical reference works) was excellent, and his international rating could not be higher. More than that, every observer could see that Pat had many more years of successful play in football. Fortunately, Pat found that the chemistry of the players at Arsenal suited him, and so what seemed like relegation was in fact more like promotion.

Coping with serious injuries

When Milija Aleksic was carried off the Manchester United field during an FA Cup replay match, he looked as if he would never walk or talk again. The injuries sustained to his face and mouth were distressing to see. A broken leg is one thing, but this was awful. Everyone knew that it was an accident, and none were more caring and concerned than the Manchester United team. The Spurs lads stayed on at a local hotel and visited him constantly. He had played so well that this seemed to be a cruel reward.

The son of a Yugoslav father, Milija was one of many fans of the late Gordon Banks. As a boy watching Stoke City, his eyes were mainly on the goalkeeper, and he cherished hopes that one day he might stand between the posts on First Division pitches. He cannot then have envisaged this shocking injury, for lads see the glory far more than they see the possible pain. However, it was remarkable that one of Britain's ablest plastic surgeons was available at Wythenshawe Hospital to give capable assistance, and so save a handsome man from permanent damage.

True to their reputation, the Spurs management ensured that Milija had the very best care until he was completely fit again, and it was thrilling to see him recover so well that he was able to be the goalkeeper at the Wembley Cup matches which followed. However, even when those exciting games were being played, it was hoped that Ray Clemence would take over in goal, in due course. The arrival of one must mean the eventual departure of the other, for this is the way that soccer works. Despite Milija's expertise on the field at Wembley, his day of departure was soon to come, for there is a limit to the number of goalkeepers even a successful club can keep. I soon discovered that sport is so different from factory or office life; the way in which players come and go has no relationship with ordinary staff appointments. Each club must make its decisions on the best advice available to it, and obtain the best players it can. Strategy and planning are key words for sports clubs which hope to succeed. To encourage Milija Aleksic to move on to another team then was not unkind; his future was wrapped up in this step. Tottenham was not relegating him – and they had given him every possible care.

The same was true of Jimmy Holmes. Soon after his recovery, he was encouraged to join a famous Canadian club, almost as if he was no longer wanted. But football is different from other sports and cannot be compared with other professions. Jimmy's injury was sustained when on international duty for his own country, in the summer of 1979. As so often happens with international sports stars, instead of sun-bathing with the rest of the team at a seaside resort, they play on. Jimmy's leg fracture was not bad, but the immediate care could have been better. In fact, if it had not been for the dedicated skill of Swiss physicians, the damage may have been lasting.

I saw Jimmy the day after he arrived back in England, where – as ever – the Tottenham club was providing expert hospital care. I was staggered by the problems that he had faced but glad that he would now fully recover. Often underrated by the fans, Jimmy had provided the Spurs with much professional talent as a sweeper. It seemed to many that we were only inviting him to leave because of the injury. The truth is that the younger lads, who were to replace Jimmy, were already sitting in the wings – and had been since before that broken leg. His move to Canada was a step in the right direction, and when he put his foot on that jet to fly there, Jimmy was in fine form.

These are but two tales out of possible hundreds. Sport is like that. Folk are coming and going all the time. Deals and negotiations are taking place whilst the rest of the world is asleep. Nothing is static for long. The lives of players (and their families) are being changed with every board meeting resolution, but how is a club chaplain to handle such things?

Encouraging the unwanted

When it became obvious to everyone but Stuart Beavon that it was time for him to move to another club in order to develop his talents, I took on the role of encourager. In many conversations, he shared his hopes and aspirations, whilst I communicated the fact that a soccer club is not a welfare centre but a business company which has to succeed on a yearly basis. When we are young, and if we are sure of our prowess, it seems right to us that everyone should be aware of their need of us. However, as Steve Perryman patiently explained to me, each player is like a chess piece and must fit in to a particular place on the field. Stuart had clear talents that were obvious to all, but I was shown one day from the viewing gallery in the gymnasium, that he would need extra talents if he played regularly in the First team, in the position that most suited Stuart. Until he acquired those extra skills, he could only be in the First team on an irregular basis, and must accept the Reserves as his usual permanent home. If Stuart hoped for better things, it was obvious that he should move on – as everyone was telling me.

Keith Burkinshaw made me a clear promise that Tottenham would do everything to help Stuart and would give him as many opportunities as possible whilst he remained with us, but he could not give Stuart a regular First team place. With that assurance, I was able to convince Stuart that it was in his best interests to take the advice he was being offered. In my own way, he was given needed encouragement and his manager was saved from having to make a personal explanation. Chaplains can do that, and so fulfil another role in the complicated manoeuvres behind the scenes in sports clubs.

A chaplain's worth?

At the close of 1983, when it was thought that a large British shipyard might close (on account of a cancelled big order), the whole of Scotland became alarmed. There were headlines in the newspapers and long interviews on television. After all, many thousands of jobs were at stake.

Who came across as the man most able to speak for the area, and most understanding of the total situation? It was the industrial chaplain for that region! So, we all had the pleasure of seeing how a chaplain can mediate outside of the usual environments of hospital and barrack room. In this same way, a sports chaplain can have just as beneficial a ministry amongst the many thousands who throng sports arenas world-wide.

5: Violence, On And Off The Field

Norman Jewison's movie *Rollerball* was intended to shock the viewer. It was planned to make us all realize that sport can be manipulated and that crowds can become violence-orientated. Set in the 21st century, and in a world that had deliberately turned its back on war and violence, the film sought to show that human nature needs an outlet for its feelings. In the film, a new sport was invented to make it possible for everyone to identify with war, without going to war, but as those who have seen *Rollerball* know, things did not turn out in quite the way that was intended.

However, all that was fiction anyway! What is the reality? What is the situation in sport right now?

How bad is bad?

At the end of September 1982, I was staying in downtown Calcutta with friends, just when the final matches were being played in the Indian soccer tournaments. As everyone in the sub-continent knows, Calcutta men are football barmy. It is their favourite sport, and they are totally involved with every move, tactic, and goal. They eat, sleep, and dream of football. If you can imagine a starry sky above, and a fascinating exotic scene below, you will appreciate how delightful Calcutta can be at the end of September, when the monsoons are over and just before the cool nights begin. This was the setting for the final game!

The last match was played and the winners declared. It was a typical cup-final atmosphere. The fans who supported the winners were jubilant and those who supported the losers were sad. However, it had been a great evening.

Suddenly, the centre of Calcutta erupted with explosions

and fires. All around the house in which I was staying, there were commotions and disorders, and they continued all night. The side which had lost was an all-Muslim team, and the side which had won was an all-Hindu team. The shops which were looted and burned (and they were not a few) were owned by the Hindustani population. It was devastatingly awful if it was sport (as we like to think of it).

However, this was not so bad as that terrible day in Peru, when 301 people died in the riots which followed a major international football match there in 1964. Compared with that, the scenes I witnessed in Calcutta in 1982 were nothing. Indeed, we see very little of real violence on the continent of Europe in sport, if we make our comparisons with the way they do things in some other countries.

The last time I was in Malta, I saw the crowd throwing stones at the players and the referee. Despite all the stories, I have never seen *that* at White Hart Lane! However, we have had our problems there, as have all stadium owners in every country.

Mindless hooliganism

The *London Times* has not made a habit of splash headlines, and so when they described some of Tottenham's supporters as 'lunatic' following a European match in Rotterdam, it may be assumed that the reporter, Clive White, really meant what he wrote. His language in the column was no softer than it had been in his title; there, he wrote of a fine English team playing against a backcloth of bombs and knife stabbings. I was not in Rotterdam that night, but it sounded a little like events in other places where I have witnessed crowd violence.

Clearly, those who attend matches can behave very badly, and their tactics after the games are sometimes unbelievable. I have stood and watched local lads climb up on to buildings in the Tottenham High Road and throw bricks down onto the heads of visitors, simply because the Spurs lost. This cannot be classed as football 'support'; these people are mindless hooligans.

The president of the Boston Bruins did a kind of arithmetical equation over vandalism and sport at one time.

Paul Mooney said that his accountants could assess in advance what the vandalism costs would be on any given night, if he knew what the final score was. Put into a few words, it goes something like this. If it is a Friday night (with the whole weekend ahead of the fans), and if the Bruins win, the total cost of vandalism is around \$500. If they lose, it is around \$5,000. If they draw (or tie), it is around \$1,000. However, if the game is on Sunday afternoon, you can halve those figures, because the crowd is 'much more sedate on a Sunday'. Not all club accountants have made such assessments, and – in any case – there are the innocent bystanders!

After three successive lost home matches at Tottenham one year, I recall seeing disgusted 'fans' urinating through the letter boxes of shops and houses in the vicinity afterwards. It was impossible to control or arrest them because of the large numbers involved. Most of those houses and shops had no links of any kind with football or sport.

Those of us who have an interest in the answer to such bad behaviour, and who have an equal interest in sport, have watched the 'supporters' and ignored the game, in order to understand the motives behind the outbursts. By doing this, and by placing myself in a position where I was able to see everything, I know that some lads attend football matches (and any other public gathering) in order to create chaos. I have watched one group of lads for the whole of one match and did not see them ever look at the football pitch! They were doing nothing other than looking for opportunities to do damage. At the close, they were the first out, and on the pavement they planned how to harm the departing fans.

Witnessing such planned violence is not easy, because the participants are full of cunning. On several occasions I narrowly escaped severe harm. More than once, I was brutally threatened. I was only trying to understand the motives so that I might make some proposals as to how best to deal with the situation, but the offenders did not want any of my interest. All who sought to breach their secrecy were in danger. It was clear then, as now, that in every country there are those who are out to create disturbances wherever the public gather in large numbers. It has nothing to do with sport.

Violence on the pitch

Some have blamed football hooliganism on the game itself, seeking to find an easy answer to a massive problem. Clearly, each match is as much a battle of skills as a game of chess is a battle of wits, but the link between violence and a goal is hard to make. This does not mean that there is no natural sequence of events when the opposing team scores, but the amateur may see links which are unreal. The problem is: how do we handle the situation that we know exists?

After weeks of studying the crowd and the changing room behaviour, I could see that the behaviour of players can affect the crowd. Equally, I realized that the fans can just as much affect the players. I have felt the surging anger in thousands of home fans if a visiting player deliberately hurts one of our lads. Otherwise sensible people, sitting near me, have become deeply affected by a deliberate foul, and have reacted violently. If thousands leave the stands feeling like that (especially if the home team loses) there is bound to be an electric atmosphere when the streets are reached.

I have been in the middle of a pitched battle on the corner of Park Lane, after such a match, and there are no holds barred. Especially when the new stand was being built, getting out of the ground, and then round and back to the Players Room was not easy. If I had been sitting amongst the visitors (because of the shortage of seats), getting through to the Tea Room was like crossing a battlefield. And, all of this was the result of a visiting player deliberately fouling one of our lads!

Over the years, and especially during the past five, I have learned to care for the players from the point of view of such 'accidents' and have watched the game where the ball *is not*. The referee's eye is on the ball, as are also those of the linesmen. If the spectators watch the players who are nowhere near the ball, they will be intrigued to discover that a lot is happening, including 'unsporting behaviour'.

Since such actions cannot be legislated against by the overworked referee, whose eyes are on the ball itself, the fans feel that the game is unfair. Without a further referee, high up in a stand, holding a video camera for proof, this kind of violence on the pitch cannot easily be contained.

The Chelsea v. Brighton match in September 1983 gave the sports reporters a lot of easy headlines because of all the violence which started many hours before the kick-off. Chelsea supporters arrived early on the Friday evening and were clashing with the Brighton fans on the sea-front, in what appeared to be a masculine demonstration of superiority that was quite unconnected with soccer. By Sunday morning, we all knew that 40 people had been badly injured, including five policemen, and 135 had been arrested. Things might have been worse if the local police had not discovered a cache of petrol bombs before noon, and if the clashes on the terraces had not been dealt with effectively. Even so, the pitch was invaded, and many innocent shoppers were hurt as the fans spilled out into the town.

However, that match is now famous for another reason. At the end of the game, one of the players, Chris Hutchings, swore at a policeman who was trying to hold back the Chelsea supporters who were seeking to invade the pitch on all sides. That policeman (PC Michael Pollett) realized that the player was using 'threatening behaviour' in a public place, and decided to pursue this through the courts. As a result, in December that year, Chris Hutchings was found guilty of an offence whilst on a football pitch, and history was made in Britain. Many of those who have been badly affected by football crowds rightly consider that this is a step in a good direction, because players must now realize that they are not above the law.

Clearly, some sportspeople have seen themselves as being 'above the law', as we saw in an earlier chapter, but the tide seems to be turning, and if more people say the right things more often, there is still hope. If every manager told his players, before every match, what Eddie Gray (of Leeds) is on record as having said, each game of soccer might be more like the game we used to know: 'Players have got to realize that they are in a position where they are idolized by thousands of supporters, and if they behave badly it can lead to crowd trouble!'

Derision and its damage

At one stage, the lads at the Spurs had one of the best teams in soccer, but could not win. Their play on the field was artistic, but they seemed to be unable to get goals. This was a difficult period to live through, and everyone on the staff was anxious. The fans felt it personally, because the visiting supporters had a wonderful time exploiting our obvious weaknesses. The songs began to have a special meaning, and the words were subtly changed to be deliberately derisive. It was not easy for the lads to go out on to the pitch during those months.

One symptom which arose during that time was uncanny. Afterwards, I was able to understand why it had happened, but at the time it seemed to be almost satanic. A large group of fans, which can always be outspoken and not a little cheeky, began to chant blasphemous remarks. I thought that I had heard all the football songs and chants (of which some are truly witty and clever), but this was all new to me. I felt that this was an undesirable turn of events which I had to tackle personally. The only tools available to me (as so often has been the case) were my typewriter and prayer. I could not speak personally to a large crowd of unhappy fans. So, after marshalling prayer support, I wrote a message to be added to the sports page of the local paper, which would be on sale at the next match. In as simple a style as possible, I appealed for restraint on the grounds of the effect that these words were having on the young lads in the team. There was an instant response, and the team recovered from its poor showing. There followed a succession of excellent games, and the tide turned.

Afterwards, I discovered that these blasphemous chants had originated in the minds of a few atheists amongst the fans who had been drinking before the game. They were likeable chaps and it had all begun as a piece of fun (whilst half-drunk). However, I found it fascinating to discover *why* it had happened, and *how* it was possible to overcome the problem. As I saw the situation then, this kind of crowd behaviour would only lead to a sort of violence that was unconnected with sport and was rather sinister. I was glad that the phase passed!

Poor refereeing

The *Malta Times* for the 6th December 1979 had the title 'Poor Refereeing' over an article about the abandonment of a match between Valetta and Florianna. The writer, Francis Mizzi, felt that referees and linesmen sometimes do not see what 'ninety nine per cent of those present at the Stadium clearly witness'. He was not the first to put pen to paper on this theme, and not the first to see a link between a referee's oversights and violence in the crowd.

Personally, I have always felt sorry for the referees and linesmen, because of the tremendous pressures upon them from all sides, and so have treated them kindly whenever we have met. Both before and after matches, I have been particularly gracious to them, regardless of the outcome of the game or their part in it. On the way home from one away match in the team coach, Keith Burkinshaw came back for a chat and we got to talking about this very subject. It was slightly embarrassing for me because I had had a long conversation with the referee and his father that afternoon, at the reception after the game. I knew that if I asked Keith how many marks he would award to *this* referee out of ten, (being a frank, outspoken Yorkshireman) he would grudgingly award one. The trouble then was, and always is, that however poor a performance each referee gives, there is no nicer chap to talk to in the Tea Room afterwards! This is because they are all sincere and want to give of their best. For them, as for the players, there are bad days and good ones. Nevertheless, as the Maltese writer correctly said, poor refereeing can create chaos, and everyone who saw that Valetta v. Florianna game is sure of that!

Patriotic resentment

Nobody has felt national resentment from a stadium crowd more than Ricardo Villa and Osvaldo Ardiles after the Argentinian invasion of the Falklands Islands in 1982. I was at Cheshunt watching the lads train on the morning that the news came through. All the newspapers wanted to know what Ricky and Ossie thought (again, they needed headlines and instant opinions). Stern measures were taken to keep the reporters away, but they still produced quoted statements. It was not easy to stop the lads teasing, or the newspapers ringing, but the manager did his best to limit the effect of the news on the performance of the team.

There is little doubt that Ossie might have done better if he had not so swiftly defended his own country, but – as he said to me – 'I have been taught from my earliest years that the Malvinas belong to my country, and that is how everyone of my generation thinks'.

The following matches were spoilt by barracking every time either of them touched the ball, and when Ossie flew out to the Argentine, in order to prepare for the international matches, Ricky had to face the jeers alone. That was a difficult time for the whole team, and spoilt a lot of games. The fans were remarkably faithful, even though local servicemen were killed in the fighting in the South Atlantic, and they welcomed Ossie back as a great hero, totally forgiving him for his remarks about the British Prime Minister. The Spurs supporters then revealed an amazing ability to behave like the perfect sportsmen they can so easily be, refusing to allow anything to spoil the game, and insisting that sport is above politics. This came across most clearly at Wembley when the lads insisted on including in the watching Ricky before they went to collect the Cup, and the fans insisted on singing 'There's only one Ricky Villa', even though he had opted not to play in order to avoid confrontations in the stands. The worst of the violence was avoided through excellent behaviour by everyone at Tottenham. It could have been very nasty!

No easy answer

Those who speak much about violence usually have pat answers if questioned as to how they would handle the situation. Those who are honest, admit that there *are* no easy answers. Since the frank observer is aware that there are many forces at work, he knows that it is a national problem requiring a comprehensive answer which embraces so many varied factors, that even governments may not be able to make a good job of it.

When we know that individual idiosyncrasies, national characteristics, personality failings, religious views, bad refereeing, poor management, lack of sports skills, jealousy, envy, pride, personal indiscipline, alcohol, drugs, lack of seating, unwise policing, and the weather, to say nothing of a shortage of tickets, can all create the wrong conditions for good crowd control, we realize that easy answers are no help.

If there is a competition taking place, and if a crowd is watching the outcome carefully, the violence which might follow need have nothing to do with sport as such. The violence which sometimes erupts in a soccer stadium can just as easily erupt at a cock fight (in those countries where such things are permitted). The problem is not in the sport, but in the human beings involved. Human nature is our enemy here. Those of us who have taken an honest look at human nature know that it is completely imperfect and cannot be perfected in this life. As a result, we know that crowd control during any form of competition will always be difficult, especially if alcohol is freely available before that competition begins. We must face up to the reality of the facts and seek a way to diminish the violence. In this world, the eradication of violence by human effort alone is impossible. However, everyone would be glad of big improvements; that ought to ensure some changes.

Who is to blame?

At one match, I was sitting high up in the West stand at White Hart Lane, next to the parents of a Leeds player, who were there to see his team win. Half way through the game, there were some scuffles in the crowd and some Tottenham supporters were removed by the police. This couple immediately began to make rude remarks about the London louts and what they would do with them, if they were allowed to set hands on them! The lady summed it all up in one final remark, before turning back to the intricacies of the match, by saying: 'I blame the parents'.

In their book *The Private Life of the American Teenager*,

child experts Myron Harris and June Norman have (remarkably) come up with the same statement. After interviewing 160,000 American young people, from coast to coast, and in every type of socio-religio-economic framework, they discovered that the overwhelming majority of American teenagers believe that hooliganism and vandalism can be blamed on the parents for not having the right standards, raising the children properly, being sufficiently caring, and being bothered. Those who are constantly saying that 'it was not like this when I was a teenager' must find some comfort in this intriguing observation by those who create the havoc we bemoan!

In 1983, Steve Perryman entered the world of journalism by having his own weekly column in the local Tottenham newspaper. He has a good style and could become a future TV anchor-man in sporting programmes if he continues with his commencing standard. Soon after he entered this new world, Steve decided to tackle the prickly subject of soccer violence and was outspokenly sensible, seeing the issues clearly. If he can influence all players to adopt his views and encourage the football authorities, the magistrates, the police, and the fans, to do the same, the situation may soon improve.

In her book *The Ancient Olympic Games*, Judith Swaddling says that the penalties were very harsh in the early centuries of international sport, if the athletes broke the rules. Perhaps the answer is to get back to the old solutions to old problems!

Government intervention

Early in 1984, the British Government published a Report on this subject of violence in sport. With all the resources at their disposal, one might have expected this to be an excellent assessment of the situation combined with a sensible answer to the problem. Instead, it was nothing but a damp squib. Apparently, the people who knew what was going on had not been involved with the compilation of the Report, and the experts on crowd control had not been invited to give their opinions. The conclusions reached in this Report were valueless. It is now obvious that solutions must come from an all-party committee, which represents all interests. The solutions must take into account the international scene, in view of the differences between the many cultures involved in world sport today.

6: Prayer And Its Influence

Arne Forsell is a freelance sports writer who lives in his native Sweden and covers all kinds of stories for a variety of newspapers and magazines, as well as taking suitable photographs to adorn his articles. He is a travelling reporter, and goes anywhere at a moment's notice in search of interesting tales for his Scandinavian readers.

One Saturday afternoon, Arne Forsell was watching the Spurs play at home in a game just before another Wembley visit, and was given a seat next to mine. During the interval, he questioned me very carefully, because he realized that I was very involved with every twist and turn of the match. He said that – if he did not think that this was unbelievable – it appeared that I was praying for the players! Arne Forsell went back to Sweden and wrote an article about 'this pastor in London who prays for footballers', and suggested that the Spurs could hardly fail to win the Cup in view of this. Fortunately, this was not read in England!

Strangely, it was a former king of Sweden who had confided, many years ago, that 'more things are wrought through prayer than this world realizes'. There never has been any secret about this. However, to pray for footballers may appear to be new, unless the reader is the parent of a footballer, because parents have prayed for their sons for centuries!

Praying for people

If it is discovered that a pastor is connected with a sports club, and especially in a country where such a thing is unusual, people's minds always turn to the subject of prayer. They see a pastor as a person who prays, and then they begin to wonder if he prays for the lads. If he does, they thinkingly inquire, *how* does he pray for them.

John Pratt, an ever-ready source of humour, tackled me about this within days of my arrival at the club. He seemed to be concerned about his near-misses when aiming at the goal mouth, and his faulty passes. 'Would prayer assist in moving the ball an extra half-an-inch?' he once asked me. John soon learned that I could pull his leg as effectively as he could pull mine!

However, in order to make everything quite clear, I did take one opportunity to explain my views on this. For me, prayer is the most remarkable of all the various forms of divine communication. It is a sensational gift which we must not misuse. On the other hand, if we don't use prayer, or adopt the attitude that it is valueless, we are missing something absolutely vital!

Arne Forsell had taken the view that prayer is for use in church on Sundays, and is too holy for a soccer stadium. I had sought to show him that he had not understood what prayer was, and so had completely misconstrued its purpose. Whilst the game went on, I told him about hearing a New York professor, over twenty years previously, give a lecture on 'Praying for Plants' and demonstrate that two boxes of bean seeds, in the same conditions, and with the same food and water supply, except that one had been prayed for by a class of students and the other had not, showed a remarkable difference. The box which had been the subject of prayer was full of more lively bean plants. 'What you can do for plants, you can do for people' was my closing line, before turning back to the game, just in time to see Glenn Hoddle take the ball through and get a goal.

The point is, *how* do we pray for people, and how can a *sports chaplain* pray for *sportspeople*, especially in such a game as football? I have never had a problem here. As I see things, footballers are *people*, and praying for people has been normal since the days of Adam and Eve. We only get confused if we think that sport is concerned just with winning, because then we see prayer as one more aid (along with training, good food, rest, and proper advice). If we see sport in those terms, then we have missed the point. Whilst it is true that in all sport there is a healthy spirit of competition (which Gary Warner has adequately assessed in his book 'Competition'), there is always a loser. It is impossible to have a sport in which there is not a loser, and so sport is not just about winning. However, it is true that to win a match is very important in commercialized sport, since only by winning can there be an assurance of good attendances.

Principles of prayer

So, as I see things, it would be wrong for me to pray that a particular team might win. I can pray for the team to play well; to be good sportsmen; to remain cool and calm; to avoid clashes; to think clearly; to keep their eyes open; to maintain the team spirit; and to be full of strength. Prayers like that are perfectly correct.

In other words, when the ball is in flight and likely to miss the goal mouth, I could not pray for it to go in anyway. Similarly, if the lads have not been persistent in their training and have cut corners with sleep, I could not pray for them to win despite negligence. We can only pray for people in accordance with certain principles, and none of these permit selfishness.

When two countries fight each other in a major war, it is more than likely that mothers on both sides will be praying for their sons in the heat of the battle. Again, they can pray only on the basis of principles and not for any selfish aim or hope. Where there is any element of competition, and where there must (of necessity) be a loser, prayer must be used with care.

Harnessing prayer

A few months after I began to get involved at Tottenham, a Christian newspaper publicized the fact and caused me a lot of problems. Other papers and magazines rang up and wanted a story, or a photograph, or both. After the pressure was off, I decided to use the interest to the advantage of the team I was with. Why not harness more prayer, by getting all these interested people involved, I thought. Little did I know what I was letting myself in for! Requests came in from all over the world asking for information and news about the Spurs team, so that the correspondents could pray for them.

Purely on financial grounds, I had to limit it to a six-monthly news bulletin, but I was amazed at the interest.

I know for a fact that the prayer support which was harnessed for the weeks prior to the 1981 and 1982 Cup Finals was colossal. Thousands of people were committed to praying for the Spurs team – and all of this quite voluntarily. There was almost a festive atmosphere in the homes of people thousands of kilometres away and on distant shores, where prayer had been offered, as the Final ties and replays were being drawn and won. During my overseas trips since those days, many have come up to me and told me that they were praying whilst those games were on.

Does this mean that Manchester City lost and the Spurs won, just because of this remarkable harnessing of prayer for two seasons of games? Certainly not! However, it does mean that the Spurs lads were wonderfully upheld during the months which led up to those matches, and during them. It must not be said that they had Heaven on their side, but (as Emlyn Hughes put it in one broadcast) at the 100th Football Association Cup Final replay, the 'Spurs were unstoppable'. Everyone who was there must have noticed the uncanny inspiration which the whole team enjoyed, and the ease with which they appeared to be able to play very skilful football right up until the last whistle.

It is possible that another chaplain would not be able to harness such a volume of prayer from so many people in quite that way. We must remember that the Tottenham Hotspur Club has an international following of considerable proportions, and by joining them I was merely attracting the attention of the Christians who were already committed fans. I only know that if anyone introduced me, at any meeting where I was speaking, as 'also being the chaplain at the Spurs' as well as doing my other work, I had a standing ovation! This is fairly rare for the run-of-the-mill pastor!

Praying for the injured

I have had lots of letters asking me if (with my views on prayer for the sick) I prayed for the injured players. My answer always was a clear 'yes'. My reputation for praying for sick people was unknown at Tottenham. In fact, when I arrived there on the first day, nobody had heard of me! So, the fact that titles have been published from my pen on the subject of healing was lost on the staff and players at White Hart Lane. In due course, I began to be recognized by visiting managers and visiting teams, but not because of what I have written on the subject of healing!

So, the first person to discover my interest was not a player but Mike Varney, the club physiotherapist, and that happened because I spoke to him about one of the chapters in his own book *The Treatment of Football Injuries*. Mike recognizes that therapies other than modern medicine have their part to play, and so he does not despise them. In fact, during his time at Tottenham, he has seen so many different requests from the players, or their families, that nothing would now be a surprise to him!

Amongst my most cherished memories are some involving hefty Spurs footballers coming up to me and asking if I will pray for themselves, their wives, or their children. It was something that I never expected would happen, back in 1949 when I turned away from industry and began life as a pastor.

And, my church has never been the same since I stopped asking them to pray for this footballer or that one. This is one area of life that we don't talk about so much these days, which the young people clearly regret!

More than coincidence?

My association with the Tottenham Hotspur lads became very intense at times, and my friends wondered if I had not become too involved! I found myself thinking about them, and wondering how they were, at all sorts of odd times. Although they sometimes felt that I was not around sufficiently, and not there when they were looking for me, we were always linked in other ways.

After one weekend away, the coach driver sought me out to tell me of an alarming experience on the previous Saturday evening. They had been speeding home from Southampton, along the motorway, and in the outside lane, when he realized that the brakes had failed. He had little time to think of much, but he thought of *me*, and realized that I could help him. It would have been more wonderful if he had said that he spent those vital seconds *thinking about the Lord*! With great enthusiasm, he told me how that he was then able to stay calm, and brought the coach to the side of the road, without any fuss, and without an accident. When I asked him the exact time, and then assured him that I had prayed about him and the coach, at that very time, he was impressed. It became clear to us both that there were links which were invisible but powerful.

Always one hundred per cent?

Every sporting club manager would love life if every player in his team was always 100 per cent fit, in body and mind. Regrettably, with human nature the way it is, that cannot be so. Even if we could eliminate all physical injuries, we are left with the emotional problems (to say nothing of all the other varieties). Some clubs have turned to various organizations in their search for lasting mental fitness, including psychotherapeutical ones. In their time, the Spurs management has had players hypnotized (and with excellent results) as well as many other things. They have also experimented with modern humanistic psychology.

The snag with some of these approaches is that they are suitable only for a few in each team, because the personality differences create barriers for this or that therapy. With one member of a team *this* works fine, but with another it has to be *that*. As a result, the desire to get the body, mind and emotions working together effectively, in 11 or 15 men – all at the same time – is frustrated. It is particularly difficult if the team ages range from 17 to 35, which is the case in most professional soccer sides today.

Despite trying to find out, I do not know if any professional team has ever employed a full-time *chaplain* to care for this side of things. It is possible that such an experiment has been carried out in America. It would be interesting to see how successful such a policy might be. One would have thought that a properly trained chaplain might be more successful in bringing the mental and emotional activities of a whole team up to peak performance than a psychologist, especially if he had a deep involvement with each member of the squad through prayer.

Stock car racing is a little more hectic than football, and full of sudden surprises. One needs to have one's body, mind and emotional activities in harmony, if one is a member of a team which is hurtling around the track in separate cars, at crazy speeds. How do the American NASCAR drivers keep cool under such pressures? Any visitor to the tracks there will find that, before the flag goes down, Bill Baird has gathered the drivers into a portable chapel, and has calmly talked to them and prayed with them. Bill is the chaplain for stock car drivers, and he has proved that his 'therapy' can work wonders.

Living in the past

When I have talked to some sports personalities about prayer, they have suggested that I am living in the past. From their point of view, this must appear to be the case. Certainly times have changed!

In the summer of 1980, I took an elderly couple out for dinner. It was his 80th birthday and they have no children to spoil them in such ways. A. J. Hale and Dorothy were predecessors of my wife and me in Wood Green. They were caring for our church in the years when bombs were falling on our heads. Mr Hale has been a life-long supporter of the Spurs and never missed a match when he was close enough to attend. A friendship grew up between him and the club, at a time when everyone needed friends. One Sunday evening, he had the whole squad in his church, for a special service. It would be a rare soccer team that agreed to such a thing these days! Times have changed, and if we think that we can have those days again, we are living in the past.

However, prayer knows no distance! And, when I was asked to pray for one of the players, or his family, I did not insist that they had to come to me. They knew that I was praying, and I knew that they were aware of it. On the other hand, when some of them did slip inside my church's doors, it was a bonus that I had not expected!

7: Involved At All Levels

Jogging, swimming, ice-skating, tennis, and horse-riding, are some of the sporting pursuits which everyone can take up, without us being involved with people we don't like. Some sports are almost personal; we can jog and pony-trek completely on our own. Other sports can be enjoyed when there is only one other person present. Football, on the other hand is not for the loner, and First Division soccer is really only for the gregarious.

In some parts of a football stadium stand we can be surrounded by a crowd of drunken hooligans, whilst in another part we may find ourselves in the middle of a group of well-educated businessmen or film stars. The company varies from row to row, and then from seat to seat. For some, this is a great drawback, because for them sport can only be enjoyed if the company is right. Hooligans are not the best neighbours if you are trying to concentrate. Also, if we must not smoke because of a lung condition, it is distressing to breathe in lots of nicotine from supporters all around, despite being in the open air.

For the well-raised lady, it can be disconcerting to have paid a lot of money for the most cherished seats and then to find that the language all around is better suited to the factory, as others nearby shout obscenities at the referee! This is the problem with any sport which attracts all kinds of people in large numbers. The most sensitive amongst us, and the deeply religious, can find the close proximity of drunken, uncouth, loud-mouthed hooligans an embarrassment, and so it is not surprising that some parents keep their children away from football grounds – in the same way that some mothers have kept their daughters away from the entertainment business. However, for the sports chaplain everyone connected with the game is a friend; he hopes to be a good influence on as many of them as possible.

At all levels

When I first arrived at the Spurs, I innocently thought that my influence was restricted to the First Team only. Within a short time, I found that the ground staff and the Reserves regarded me as belonging to them also. Before the year was out, I saw the whole crowd as a potential circle of friends! I found myself mixing with people that I had not been among for years, and having long conversations with characters that I had never mixed with before. This is not to say that I had led a sheltered life, but pastors can be limited in the kind of people that they visit and speak to. This leads to them having a special language which is unworldly and precise. The rough and tumble language of the blue collar London football supporter is completely different. I had to learn what *not* to say and *how* to say what I wanted to say. For a Yorkshireman, this was not easy!

I tried to make a habit of visiting every player, member of staff, or director, when they were in hospital. Early on, I had to do this for Ricky Villa. Unfortunately, I chose a time when his parents and wife were also there, and so I had the problem of trying to say the few Spanish words that I then knew in between the flow of conversation. My knowledge of a few more Portuguese words made things even more complicated because it seemed to them that I was speaking Argentinian Spanish with an odd accent! However, they knew that I had been bothered enough to go out of my way and make that visit.

On outings, the club always insisted that I should eat with the directors (in the same way that padres eat with the officers), and I missed not only a lot of fun but also a lot of opportunities. It is strange how people think that they know what you would prefer, and what is best for you!

Chris Hughton is now a famous international soccer star, with a fine reputation for a steady standard of play, but I remember him when he was a lad in the Reserves. On the Friday when he was chosen to fill a gap and play for the second time in the First Team, he was a little apprehensive. When the lads came out of the changing room after training, I took him through into the Tea Room and looked after him, before it was time to climb into the coach. I sat him down, talked kindly, made him toast, poured out tea for him and cared for him generally. Some of the lads wondered what this meant! Chris is the son of a mixed marriage, and so draws strength from both European and African blood, but he was in need of all the encouragement that anyone could give him that day. It was a make-or-break experience. If he failed in this game, he would never rise out of the Reserves, but if he did well he may never go back to them. It cost me nothing to behave like a butler, and give Chris the encouragement that he needed, and if a chaplain is to fulfil his role properly, he must be like a servant on many occasions.

Wives and girlfriends

Many times it has been said that behind every famous man there is a good wife. With soccer players now getting younger, this is less likely to be the case, but the principle remains true. Jimmy Greaves has been frank enough to admit that his marriage break-up was his fault and that he did not appreciate his wife sufficiently when she was there. Glenn Hoddle has also admitted that marriage to the right girl gives a footballer 'the stabilising influence of a settled home'. It is clear that a steady relationship is vital for every professional person, and especially for sportspeople. The gossip columns of the newspapers assure us of this.

Getting young lads to see this is never easy, for they all want to keep their options open for as long as possible. A sports club needs to make all the girlfriends welcome on every possible occasion, and thus help to cement the relationships or show up the weaknesses in the friendships. More than once, one of the lads confessed to me that when he saw his girlfriend next to the wives of the manager and senior players, he realized that she was the wrong choice. The standards set by wives like Joyce Burkinshaw, Cheryl Perryman, Sylvia Ardiles, Anne Hoddle, and Marie Pratt are high, and give a very clear picture of what a footballer's wife can be like. Seeing these established wives has been a help to many a young sportsman and shown him that wives have a role to play in the sport, as well as in the home.

At Tottenham, this was fully realized, and so the lads were encouraged to bring their wives and girlfriends to as many games as possible and to all the social events. This gave me a chance to meet them, introduce myself, and try to build up a relationship. There was some resistance at first, because the girls wondered why this clergyman wanted to chat them up, but they warmed to me in due course. I ended up by having long conversations with some of them about all sorts of domestic situations, when it became obvious that I was not some sort of staff spy!

It is one of the clear rules of chaplaincy that there must be complete confidentiality all round. This is just as true in sport as it has been traditionally in the armed services, the entertainment industry, hospitals and prisons. Wherever chaplains talk to people, everything said must remain private. For this reason, the majority of the fascinating stories known to every chaplain cannot by publicized. If the rule is broken once, there will be no hope for future chaplains in any sphere, and certainly not amongst the wives and sweethearts.

In all weathers

Some sports supporters follow their team only when the weather suits them, and often for good reasons. In the crowd, I have met retired footballers who still watch the game, but because of old injuries or arthritis, they don't venture out in the cold winds or when it is raining. Young supporters have no such wisdom, and so they watch the games improperly dressed, and with no thought for their future health.

A chaplain *must* be there, whatever the weather. During the winter months, standing on the windswept training ground at Cheshunt, I learned how to keep as dry and warm as possible in the pouring rain. Many times, I have dashed from there to a café on the A10, to have some hot soup, in order to keep my temperature up, before the days when the Spurs had their own built-in café for post-training snacks.

When the sun was hot, the situation was reversed, and keeping cool was as difficult as keeping warm in the winter. With cameras around, Keith Burkinshaw didn't mind being stripped to the waist, but I had to try to maintain some sort of dignity!

To and from Wembley

All over the world, there is an enthusiastic interest in the happenings at Wembley. Amongst football supporters, the major soccer events at Wembley are held in the highest honour; some speak of those games in hushed tones. One of my most intriguing memories is of a lively young man coming up to me in Northern Bengal and asking if I had ever been to watch a match at Wembley. He put the question in such a way that he expected me to say 'no', because he had never met anyone who had been, and he did not expect that he ever would go. When I told him that I had been there three times in the previous season, he appeared to be about to faint, and then clung to me as if the nostalgia of those games would be transferred to him. If I had been Stanley Matthews, I could not have had a warmer reception from this lad and his friends!

Getting to and from Wembley can be as exciting as being inside the ground, because the build-up to it, and the excitement after it, is quite unique. On one occasion, I travelled through from Seven Sisters by underground trains all the way, in the midst of thousands of avid supporters, who sang themselves hoarse before we got there. The scenes in the trains were reminiscent of those I witnessed on VE night, many years before. There was the same boisterous enthusiasm, and happy good-natured liberality.

On another occasion, my wife and I travelled north of Wembley by car, had a leisurely lunch in a quiet village, and then travelled south on a train which was devoid of supporters (because they were all going in the other direction). That approach was placid until the Wembley Station was reached! There, in an instant, we were plunged into the general mêlée, and almost carried through to the stadium without putting our toes on the pavement.

The most fascinating way to travel to and from Wembley is to be in the cavalcade of coaches, with the players. On the way home from a winning match, the streets all the way are lined with people waving, as if it was a royal tour of Kenya. As the coaches reach the boundaries of Tottenham, the cars, buses, and cycles, ring and sound every kind of horn and bell available to them, adding to the cacophony of welcome from the thousands who have taken to the streets. If it were not for the large numbers of police on duty, the stars of the day never would reach the doors of the home ground, and the welcoming arms of their wives. To be allowed into this private celebration, and to be included as one of the staff after such a famous international win, is a privilege that few sports chaplains have shared, but all envy.

In the off-season

Some people think that there is nothing to do at a football club when the gates are closed and everyone is on their summer vacation. Just because the season is over does not mean that nothing is happening. I learned at Tottenham that the place can be a hive of activity behind the scenes when the lads are not around. This is the only time to put paint to property, and to do the necessary building work that must be finished by the time that the gates re-open to the next season's crowds. It is also the only time that the ground staff can put in hand the vital jobs connected with the pitch and stands.

The White Hart Lane ground is one of the best furnished and maintained in British football. The facilities are comparable with the best in North America, especially now that they have the modern West Stand with all of its luxurious rooms and boxes. It is also one of the best grounds in the country with natural turf. During my time there, this was due to the indefatigable services of Colin White, who cared for that grass like a nurse cares for her patients. He had a relationship with the turf, almost talking to it and encouraging it to grow better. Because of such faithfulness from all of the ground staff, from those employed full-time down to those who did just a few hours when the team played at home, I visited the club each week even when the gates were closed, just to be seen there and to chat with those who were around. This resulted in friendships that I could never have dreamed of once upon a time, and gave me new insights into what makes a major sporting club 'tick'.

Ambassador extraordinaire

When a chap like me gets his ticket for Wembley Stadium for

the major soccer event of the year, he gets to wondering who he will be sitting next to, and what the conversation will be like. Because of *why* I had the ticket, and *who* I represented, I saw my role there (to those sitting around me) as a diplomatic one; it was important that I said the right things.

One year, and when my wife Doreen was not with me, I discovered that my neighbour was a young and beautiful film-star! Obviously, this was not the time to open up a conversation about why the regular supporters cannot get tickets when their team goes to Wembley but the likes of film stars can! Also, it was not diplomatic to tell her that I had seen her in a late night TV play, only a few days previously, where she appeared completely naked for a few seconds! I talked with her, but never mentioned her career, or mine. The conversation was about understanding the game, the problems facing each player, and the reason behind each decision of the referee.

Only as we parted company did I introduce myself, and explain what my role was. I did not wait for her reaction, and thought that in her own profession she has as many if not more obstacles to face.

After-care

When Darryl Stingley discovered that he was a quadriplegic to the doctors, he did not even know what the word meant. He had to ask a nurse for a definition. When he discovered that it meant that his body would not function correctly from his shoulders down, and that he would never play for the Patriots NFL team again, he went into a deep depression. This depression was one of those which makes the patient antagonistic to everything. For days, nothing was right for him, and no visitor could please him over anything. It looked as if he would go into a decline and ebb away.

Fortunately, there was a doctor at the Chicago Rehabilitation Centre who understood what it is like for a football star to have an early retirement from the game through serious injury and he guided Darryl through the mental intricacies of accepting the world the way that it is, and getting the most out of it whilst we are alive. Dr Vinod Sahgal is one of those kindly physicians who has time for the difficult cases, and he pulled Darryl through.

Those who have the task of helping injured sportsmen to cope with major challenges would do well to read Darryl's story in his book *Happy To Be Alive*, because there is no easy answer for those who must quit the game early, on account of an accident. Darryl now lives in a specially refurbished apartment in downtown Chicago, and is attended daily by a nurse and a therapist. Helping others to cope is a major task in every pastor's life, and it cannot be avoided in a sporting club. There, the trauma can be worse than in any other area of life, or profession.

The effect on others

A news reporter went up to several of the players one day to ask what they thought of having a chaplain attached to the club. *Paul Miller* said, 'I like having David around. I have not had to call upon him for help personally, but I know those who have. For me, it is like having an insurance policy, seeing him sitting in the stand.' *Gary Brooke* said, 'For me, Dave is a father-figure friend, with all that implies.' *Steve Perryman* said, 'In each team, there must always be those who look after the body – the trainers and physiotherapists. But it is just as important that we have someone on hand to look after the spiritual side. Dave does that.'

Links with the staff

It is the same for chaplains in every profession: they seem to belong to 'the others'. If you are a non-commissioned soldier, the padre is like an officer, but to the officers, a padre is like a private. The players always spoke to me as if I was one of the directors, and classed me with them, but the directors did not see me as being one of them. This resulted in me feeling that I did not belong to any group really! In a hospital, the chaplain is just as much a 'piggy in the middle' as in sport or industry. By trying to help all, but through not belonging to any, every chaplain has a kind of tightrope existence. He cannot hope to please many for long, and knows that he will upset a lot during his career. In view of this, I did not do badly.

I quickly learned that every player, and every member of the staff (including myself) must not argue with any of the directors or the club manager about anything. British football is different from any other sport, and different from any other kind of industry. There is an element of feudalism in it, which I had not fully appreciated before, not having been on the inside. My training had not prepared me for this completely different approach to the way of running things. All of my experience in factories was of no avail; football in the UK is truly 'a different ball game'.

I had been there only three weeks when one of the directors opened up a conversation with me on the subject of punishment. It followed on from the latest news about vandalism, and this gentleman went on to assert that the punishment must always suit the crime, and that magistrates were too lenient. I was happy to agree with this until he quoted the case of a middle-aged lady who had stolen goods from a shop and been released without a fine and only a caution. If we had stayed on the problem of football vandalism, we would have been all right, but I was foolish enough to get involved in this conversation which had now gone off at a tangent. I ended up by stating the case for mercy in such cases, and was roundly condemned for being soft on crime! He never did speak to me again, even though I tried to be polite. I had made the mistake of arguing with one of the directors of a British football club. After that, I understood the principles better!

Helping in crises

I was on the coach, and sitting opposite Glenn Hoddle, after an away-match against Queens Park Rangers, on Boxing Day, at the end of 1979. He was unhappy and clearly thinking through the words he was going to use as soon as he got the chance. Glenn had just passed through an exciting six months, which included his marriage to Anne and offers from overseas clubs, but then – apparently without warning – he was dropped from the First team. This did follow a crashing defeat at home to Arsenal, but Glenn did not know that he would not be playing against QPR until just before the start of the game. That was bound to upset any lad as young as Glenn was then. Before we got off the coach, I twice told him not to argue with the manager whatever else he did. Glenn has been brave enough to put on record in his own book, the fact that, literally, as he stepped off the coach, he tore into Keith Burkinshaw and demanded a transfer away from Tottenham. I stood quietly, as they talked together, witnessing tense moments which resulted in Glenn not playing for the next three games. Since he has publicized this incident, through the newspapers and in his book, it is permissible for me to quote it here, as an illustration of the situation.

Glenn is one of those lads everyone likes, and his apparent relegation had to be short-lived because the fans would not have approved of anything else, but – like the rest of us – he had to learn that the manager is the boss in British football, and there is no sense in arguing with him about the way he runs his club. Personally, I thought that the manager was right to keep Glenn back for that one game at QPR, and if Glenn had not argued and stayed away from training the next day (having not played on Boxing Day), he would have been back in the First Team the following week. It is not easy to be a star player with international qualities (which Glenn has had from an early age), and be willing to accept the word of the manager, especially if you feel that he might be wrong! However, that is the way football works, and we all have to live with it. It is to Glenn's credit that he has learned.

It's nothing like marriage!

When young people become marriage partners, they have to learn to live with one another. This involves a lot of 'giving and taking', as well as patient understanding and tolerant care. The result of years of such marriage-blending is that two people are able to live with each other in a loving relationship, despite being aware of each other's failings.

Sport is quite different, because here ability and success are everything. If a player does not fit in with the rest of the squad, or if his talents fail him, he must be replaced. There can be little generosity, because the game cannot spare time and money on those who are square pegs in round holes.

So, whereas in a marriage we do everything in our power to

keep the couple together, by careful counselling, in sport there is no room for such a ministry. The cut and thrust of commercial sport make it nothing like marriage. On the other hand, it is in the interest of everyone involved that each sport continues to attract sizeable crowds. For this reason, every player must come to terms with the situation in each sport and adapt to it. The result of this is that sport becomes a little like show business, where everyone is loving towards everyone else, even though the others are all after your job!

The tension coupled to the attraction make commercial sport special; it cannot easily be compared to anything else, and those in it (and especially the players) are in a unique situation. They already have our cheers when they are successful; they need our sympathy when things go wrong.

8: Pre-match And Post-match

Those of us who have attended the celebrations which follow a rugby win, know *what* those lads get up to. Judging by what I know of Yorkshire cricket, through my cousin, post-match celebrations amongst sportsmen are pretty much the same, all over Europe! The renowned 19th hole in golf is but the open mouth of the exhausted player, and judging by their use of this 'last' hole, one might be tempted to think that golfers only set off from home in order to get to the club-house as quickly as possible. Back home, the deserted wife feels that her husband's sport is her main rival.

Knowing the social side of sport, and the likely train of events at any post-match celebrations, many have written to ask me how I could be a chaplain to a football club. The answer is no different from any that would be given if the words 'football club' were deleted and 'hospital', 'factory', or 'army' substituted. Christmas Eve in a hospital can be an eye-opener for any sensitive new nurse, and the same applies to some factory parties that I have attended! The difference is that if a team wins every other home match, and gets a long way in the run-up to the national trophies, there will be more celebrations than one might expect in the average hospital, prison, army, or factory!

Before each match

On one coach journey, as the team travelled miles north of London, some of the lads decided to relieve their boredom by playing a few tricks on me. As it so happened, I had not been able to get any sleep the night before and so playing tricks on me that day was easy. They gathered all around to watch me be made to look like a fool, and then – to press home their point – they brought in Osvaldo Ardiles, to show that if he (not even an Englishman) could understand their puzzle, I must be a right nut! It was all good fun, and so successful that one of the directors complained that I was making the players too light-hearted (and too noisy) before the match! I took the view then that anything which relieved tension was a good thing, because young men can become nervous about a big away-match.

On another occasion, several of the lads came up to me and said, 'Dave, we are worried about one of the players. He is really depressed and this is an important game. You are the only person who can help him. Please go and talk to him.' Immediately, I disbelieved the story and presumed that it was another trick and part of their pre-match tension humour. Promising to deal with it straight away, I first ran a check with the manager and trainer, both of whom assured me that the player was in good form and not at all depressed.

I then made a special point of appearing to approach the needy young man, in full view of those who had asked me to 'help' him, and proceeded to talk to him in the most animated way that I could summon up. From a distance, it looked as if I was having a serious conversation with someone who had a great need for psychological care. In fact, we were talking about the subject which he cherished most of all, apart from football! Later, they asked him 'what Dave had been spending such a long time' talking to him about, and discovered that I had been able (on that occasion) to turn the trick on to them. I learned that if you put twelve young men together and tell them that they are going to set off on an exploit that will not be easy and that they may not win, nervous tension is bound to be created. Fun is one way to relieve the tension without lessening the readiness of the team. I did not mind being the source of that fun!

When they played at White Hart Lane, I made sure that I was there with them during the training the day before. When they were playing away from home, I made sure that I was there to see them off in their coach, talking to each one and waving them all off. If I wasn't with them, they knew that I was involved enough not to forget them. Sunshine or rain, hail or snow, I was usually there!

After each match

Each major sports club has its own rules about who can, and who cannot, reach the team after a match. It is traditional for the manager to talk to his team at the end of each game, and also for the news reporters to chat with those they wish to interview. After that, each club is different, and the differences are often due to the premises available. If there is plenty of room for a lot of fans to be entertained, and if club funds permit, those staying on at the ground to celebrate a win might amount to a very large number.

In British football, the wives of players who are free to travel will tell us which clubs have the best facilities and which offer the best food after a game. There is almost an element of rivalry about it, as top clubs seek to do as well as Manchester United, or Liverpool. Each newcomer to the First Division has to face this new challenge, on top of the bigger problem of staying in the First Division.

The various football chaplains have to find a place in all of the varieties of celebrations that are going on. Do they go with the directors (with whom they might have had lunch), or with the relatives and friends, or do they go into the Players' Room to be with the lads? In most clubs, the chaplains are not allowed into the Directors' Room (despite earlier fraternities), and in some clubs, they are not allowed into the Players' Room. This does not leave much choice! They usually end up talking to wives and fathers (if not brothers and girlfriends) of the players from both sides, in a room set apart for those who are neither players nor directors.

At the Tottenham Hotspur Club, we are fortunate, because these things have been considered, and because precedents have been set. Not only that, but the premises are adequate for any eventuality under the title of 'celebrations' after a match. So, armed with a suitable pass, I was able to mingle freely with anyone, and go into almost every corner of the buildings.

I considered that it was my duty always to be in the tunnel leading to the changing rooms at the close of play, so that anyone could speak to me who felt that they would like to do so. The young players who had been involved in some difficult play, knew that the reporters were waiting for them. I tried to speak to these and prepare them for what I had heard that the reporters wanted to ask. On a very few occasions, I spirited the players out and away so that they did not come into contact with the sports writers until after they had had time to think through what they did, and did not, want to say to them.

Standing there, and waiting patiently, I often had chats with the players and staff from the visiting teams. This way, I developed a nodding acquaintance with hundreds of famous footballers and their managers.

Sometimes stars of the stage and screen would be brought through from the field by this route and then I ended up chatting to the likes of Peter Cooke, Dudley Moore, 'Alf Garnet', and Chas and Dave. On one occasion, a leading British club had been playing the Spurs at Tottenham and they had lost. This was a rare event for the visitors, and so the celebrations at White Hart Lane were noisy. The visiting players did not relish the thought of going into the Players' Room, and their most celebrated supporters had driven off well ahead of the last whistle, in order to avoid any challenge from the reporters.

I was standing there, waiting for all the Spurs lads to filter through, when their manager came up to me and said that I was the very chap he was looking for. He asked me if I could get him out of the building and into the waiting coach, past the reporters, and without anybody seeing him leave. I said that I could, but the reporters had particularly asked everyone to make sure that they were able to interview *him*. The reply was very much to the point: he particularly wanted to get onto the coach unnoticed. I got him there!

Doing favours became a way of life, and the number of people who asked me to get them autographs (only to be told that I never did that) was huge. I had to learn how to say 'no' without appearing to be unkind, and how to be pleasant to those who were being completely unpleasant to me!

After Wembley

The two wins by the Tottenham Hotspur team at Wembley in 1981 and 1982, were the result of replays. This meant that the arrangements for the possible Saturday wins were not fulfilled. The real celebrations were after the evening replays, late at night, in Tottenham. Although both wins were, because of the delay, not as exciting as they might have been, they were thrilling for the fans at Tottenham. This team had known defeat; they had been relegated to the Second Division; they had passed through several years of uphill struggle, seeking to rid themselves of the traditions of the past, and enter the 1980s with a new-look form of football which would bring back the crowds and attract whole families. The credit for this long haul back to fame and good fortune must be given to Keith Burkinshaw, Peter Shreeves, Steve Perryman, and the other members of staff. They worked hard to turn round the aspirations of the players and to bring hope to the faithful fans. I know how much effort they all put into the venture of seeking to climb back up the ladder of success and try for the prize of three Finals in a row.

These were real celebrations; they were a sort of relieved effervescence. It was spontaneous joy. Everybody loved everybody else, in such a wholesome way that it closely resembled an old-fashioned Love-Feast. I was sorry to leave before the end, because (unlike lots of them) I had to be at work a few hours later, for tomorrow had already arrived! My fondest memory of those celebrations in 1981 was of sitting at a table with Garth Crooks and his friends, and hearing him repeat 'I have seen my name in lights at Wembley.' He was like a little boy, enrapt with a vision. He was not alone with such feelings!

9: The Media And Its Messengers

I was not chosen for the role of chaplain at Tottenham because of my links with journalism. They did not then know that I had a union card as an author, and I am not sure that they were happy when they discovered it!

Newspaper reporting has gained a bad reputation over the past two hundred years, because of the unfortunate ability that some writers have to invent tales which they know will please the readers. We have known for more than a century that we cannot believe everything that we read in the newspapers, but the effect of invented news upon young and rising professional people can be devastating. This is particularly true if the subject of the news item is living away from home and family. That is the situation for many young First Division footballers.

When you know the person involved and are aware of all of the facts, the words that you read after publication are sometimes so shocking that anger is a normal reaction, until you realize that publicity is never bad for the rising stars.

Publicity is never bad

For the young and inexperienced, a false story is a sickening experience, and so I made it a habit to talk to those about whom the reporters were writing that day. If the papers were full of praise, there had to be a warning that it might be the opposite next week, and if the writers were criticizing, some encouragement was necessary.

It helps a young sportsman to understand how a writer ticks, and then he will appreciate why the newspapers so often get it wrong. After all, the reporters are human too, and they understand about emotions and hurt feelings. When the whole business of journalism is explained, and after a young footballer has grasped why there is a need to fill so many inches of newspaper each day (even if there are no stories to write about), life becomes more bearable. Each has his job to do, and the public demands that there is news. If they are not reading about Princess Diana, they would like to get the latest in the George Best saga.

When it is explained to the rising stars of the sports field that they are like the film stars of yesterday, and so their lives and loves are as interesting today as those of Elizabeth Taylor were yesterday, they can bear it better. To this extent, all publicity is good. After all, the reporters will not be fighting their way to our doors if we are no longer in the public eye! Their interest is proof that we are still attracting attention. When the newspapers stop phoning, we shall know that the public has lost interest.

Getting it wrong

The writers rarely got everything right whilst I was at the Spurs, and some of the things they wrote (and even after a recorded interview) were pure fiction. One of the worst was in connection with the 1981 Centenary FA Challenge Cup Final at Wembley. Tottenham was playing Manchester City, and Her Majesty, the Queen Mother, was watching. Our lads gave the impression that they wished to display all of their talents to the best advantage, whilst the Manchester lads made sure that the Tottenham players did not have time to do this. In order to try and obtain a win, the Spurs manager substituted Ricky Villa. As it happened, even this did not upset the balance, but it was a perfectly normal and understandable piece of strategy. Ricky took it badly and walked out to the changing room looking like a classical case of depression.

Instead of asking anybody and instead of getting the true story, one writer went into great detail as to how I had gone into the dressing room and sat with Ricky, holding his hand, and pouring in encouragement. At that match, I was in a stand seat right through until the last whistle! The tale was pure invention.

Unfair tactics

The problem with some forms of journalism is that it has no concern for those who are the subject of the article. I was more anxious about the people involved than the editor's demands, but all journalists cannot be expected to feel similarly. Getting a good story comes before compassion for most.

Nevertheless, I was angry when the tabloid newspapers released a story about one of our young players just at a time when it was vital that he should be left alone. The story suggested that he was communicating with spirit healers in connection with his injuries and a transfer to another club. The articles even gave the suggestion that his marriage needed this kind of assistance as well. Considering that his marriage was very new at the time, that he was not injured when the article was written, and that even the bits that were true were two years old anyway, this story was in very bad taste. I was very suspicious that the article was written deliberately in order to upset the anchor man in a team that needed to progress and could not afford to play badly. If there isn't any bribery amongst journalists, this tale went a long way to give the opposite impression.

Getting everybody in sport to 'put their house in order' is asking for too much. Human nature has affected it, in too many ways, for far too long, but that does not stop people like chaplains shouting when there are unfair tactics.

Loving sports writers

When the BBC announcer says, 'And, now we are going over to Wimbledon', we can be pretty sure that the voice which then hails us from the Centre Court will be that of Gerald Williams, because he has become so much a part of the scene, and such an expert on international tennis, that Wimbledon on the radio without Gerald is unthinkable.

Tennis fans worldwide have become envious of Gerald Williams because not only does he see all the action, at all the tournaments, but he meets all the tennis stars as well. I first met Gerald at Tottenham, because he is just as proficient at football commentating. In fact, he has been involved with both tennis and football from the earliest years, having been reared in a home which was close by the Upper Norwood tennis courts and the Crystal Palace's Selhurst Park. As a boy, these were his favourite sports and he only knew that he wanted to become a sports writer. Whilst I was living in Leicester, and studying engineering at Loughborough, Gerald was on the local 'Mercury' writing about the happenings at Filbert Street (where my brother Frank and I would have been a part of the crowd).

Discovering that Gerald was a Christian helped me to see the other reporters in a better light. Having such a trustworthy writer amongst them, somehow made the whole barrel more acceptable; I began to see them all as potential helpmates. However, none of the others ever became quite so friendly! At the drop of a hat, and in the middle of something important, or in the presence of eminent people, Gerald would come over and hug me and say how much he thanked God for putting me in this work. His professionalism never seems to be affected by his sheer love for life and for people. Now that he has set down his story in his book *A Whole New Ball Game*, everyone can read about this delightful fellow, who helped me to love sports writers!

Another of the commentators in British sport is John Motson. His father was a Methodist minister, back in the days when I had belonged to the Methodists. His father was at Cambridge at the same time as the Hon. Roland Lamb; as a lad, these were amongst those I respected in that denomination. I was thrilled to know that John gave me that link with the past, and I was never better pleased than when John travelled with the Spurs team on their coach to their away-matches, in order to cover the game for BBC TV. His remarkable memory and persistent study of all the features of every game makes him a newsman par excellence, and give the sports media an improved image. His article in the Steve Perryman Testimonial Programme was not only an example of good writing: it was an excellent style for others to copy!

Pitfalls for reporters

When one of my forebears, John Rushworth, set in hand to write a complete record of the English Civil War, in his

Historical Collections, he could not have known that this would lead to him being arrested by Charles the Second and kept under lock and key until his death. When most authors put pen to paper, they do not know what reaction there will be, or how much animosity will be stirred up. The majority are thinking more about how pleased the editor will be and how much they will be paid. A few may have hopes of lasting fame, but the average author has a burden to commit to print the words that flow through his mind in such a way that there will be a sufficient reward.

In my own sports column, I have known what it is to take a lot of trouble to get my facts right, and then ask whoever had been interviewed to read through the draft article, but still be reprimanded afterwards by those who had changed their minds! Because this will continue to be true, we know that sports reporters will be blamed even when they are innocent. There are many pitfalls for every journalist, and they will not lessen with the advent of instant reporting for use in international telecommunications. It is the deliberate invention which embitters the innocent victim, and we don't have to be sportsmen or sportswomen to know that!

Leif Johansson is a talented writer in Scandinavia and his work is to be praised. However, he really excelled himself in one article for a journal in his own country when he announced what I would be doing at the Spurs in the future. He entered the realm of prophecy, which even gifted clergymen do not hurry into! If the 'prophecy' had been based on sound information, it would have been understandable, but nobody could remember having thought such a thing, never mind having either said it or decided it! Does this mean that wishful thinking is now permissible amongst sports writers? If so, we may have problems of a kind greater than we have known previously. What I do know is that this article did nothing to help forward the cause of sports chaplaincies, and that was a pity!

Sir Patrick Neill wrote in the Foreword to the British Press Council's 27th Annual Report, 'Editors, and all employed in the procurement of news, ought to exercise both their intelligence and their humanity to recognise situations in which it is wrong, and perhaps sometimes almost indecent, to pursue stricken individuals with questions which they have already refused to answer. This is not to advocate that the Press should cease to be vigilant, to expose crime, malpractice and incompetence; it is an exhortation to temper zeal with discrimination and sensitivity.'

10: Encouraging The Fans

Considering that I have had years of graffiti messages about the Spurs on my garage doors, it is remarkable that I can speak affectionately about the folk who daub the paint. However, I know for a fact that football fans are amongst the most likeable people that one could meet. The fact that a few hooligans have given them a bad name, does not affect the situation. In every profession, there are those who are corrupt, but the majority carry on with their reputable duties. Football fans are no different from the rest.

In fact, the international commentators who have derided football fans on account of the vandalism which has made headlines, are living in a self-created artificial world. In every realm of life, the majority are law-abiding citizens who are as angry about the lunatic minority as the magistrates. Despite what has been said in the earlier chapter about violence, I have only felt threatened a few times amongst the fans after a match, outside the ground. That is the testimony of the overwhelming majority who have ever been to a soccer stadium.

It has been my pleasure to work with a club which knows this to be the case, and so has done everything possible to make the fans happy, and to turn each home game into a memorable event for the whole family. Regardless of misunderstandings, to my certain knowledge, there never has been a time when the well-being of the fans was ignored, or when their comfort was deliberately set aside. At Tottenham, the fans are wanted and are welcomed.

Extending a welcome

Whenever large numbers of people are involved, there is a major problem. How will they all get to the ground? Will the fans from the opposing clubs be allowed to mix together or be separated? Will the toilet facilities be sufficient? Will the refreshments be available to all? Will the tickets be correctly allocated? These are only a few of the many questions that must be asked before a major event is proposed. Then, even with the best planning, and the most efficient stewarding, there will be some mistakes and there will be those who are upset for no sensible reason.

Extending a welcome to a huge crowd, week after week, without growing stale, and without being over-disciplined, is one of the most difficult challenges we are ever likely to meet. Very few can do it well. If the stewards are not under proper control, fans can be lost in large numbers through overbearing behaviour. The same is true for the ticket attendants, the programme sellers, the refreshment sales-girls, and all the others.

It is possible that I met more of the crowd each Saturday than many of the staff. Because each has his or her duties (and the majority of the staff have their work to do within the offices), they are limited as far as real contact with the average fan is concerned. As soon as the Spurs team was inside the changing room, I was free to mingle with the crowd. Some days, I would go into the various local cafés; other days, I would go amongst the visiting fans to chat with them; on the rest of the days, I would go onto the terraces, or into the stands, talking with as many of the Spurs fans as there was time for, before I had to take my seat for the kick-off.

By wandering about like this, I did nothing to enamour myself with the stewards who did not know me, but I felt the heartbeat of the average fan on both sides. This kind of 'mixing with the crowd' was warmly welcomed. I got the impression that such things had not happened before. It reminded me of some factories, where the staff are separated from the blue collar workers, and each knows little of the other. Fortunately, I had been trained in factories where there were no such divisions, and my own father had taught me the elements of good management out of his own considerable experience. Obviously, the directors cannot mingle with the hooligans before and after each game, but somebody ought to, and then the board meeting will be able to have that point of view on its agendas. The Spurs directors get this kind of feedback.

All sorts and sizes

The advantage of a major club like Tottenham Hotspur is that it attracts all kinds of fans, from all walks of life. When the Minister of Sport talks in public about the bad behaviour of soccer fans, one presumes that he is not including the film stars, judges, company directors, politicians, accountants, barristers, and clergymen that I have seen sitting in the stands near me. This is the trouble with generalizations; they over-simplify the situation. Soccer fans are a many-splendoured company.

It can be a surprise to see James Garner shouting the lads on, until you remember that he is only an actor, and is not a Californian private eye full-time! In the same way, it would be wrong to assume that all of the fans of the top British soccer clubs are *British*. Quite often, I found that people sitting next to me could not speak a word of English, and had flown in by charter flight just to see the match.

There is a great need for careful public relations with all of these groups in view of their potential (in terms of the future spectators). More than once, I found myself helping an overseas visitor who had upset a steward, and was about to be evicted or reprimanded. Where diplomacy was needed, the older stewards always excelled, but the younger ones were more nimble and more aware of the intricacies of a multi-national crowd.

The day before one of the Wembley games, an overseas fan came to see me and told me how he had been boasting about his ticket in a London public house and someone had snatched it from his hand and stolen it. He had been to the Tottenham ticket office and they had told him (quite correctly) that it was nothing to do with them, because they had handed it over and he was not on the Spurs property when he lost it. He asked me to help. By careful diplomacy, I got this fellow into the Wembley Stadium, and there he was posted to watch the empty seat and then wave to the police. He got his seat, the police got their man, and we had a grateful fan. To my certain knowledge, that kind of friendship is being extended all the time. Football fans are no different from any other group, and they are remarkably faithful.

Football mad!

One fan who attracted my attention was a girl of about 20 years who arrived at all the games early, utterly covered in souvenir scarves and stickers, and gave the distinct impression that she was totally hooked on the Spurs. She found out who I was, and from that day I was Dave to her and to all her family. In my innocence, I thought that she was some unintelligent girl who had got nothing better to do than be a soccer devotee. One day, at Cheshunt, she told me where she lived, and I realized that she did a round trip of almost 250 miles to see the home matches. On one occasion when she was in a talkative mood, I asked her if she had a job, and she said 'Yes.' After some persuasion, she told me that she was a pathological laboratory technician with a degree in medicine. Seeing her standing there, awash with Spurs regalia, it was difficult to imagine her examining human tissue, but a few test questions assured me that this was her job. Like hundreds of others, she became a close friend.

At another ground, and obviously with less-trained stewards than at Tottenham, I know of a fan who had what was obviously a heart attack just as he was going through the turnstile. The fan behind him, who was also well decked-out in a team tee-shirt, cap, and scarf, immediately offered to give cardiac treatment. The steward waved him back and told him to leave the fellow alone. The animated young fan said 'But I am a cardiac specialist!' The steward replied, 'I know! And I am the Queen of Sheba! Keep away, I will send for an ambulance.' Upon arrival in hospital, the man was dead, and the exuberant fan really could have made a proper medical attempt to save his life.

In our church, everyone is equal as soon as they come through the doors. Status is left behind, as we form a fellowship in worship. It is just the same in a sports stadium. Inside, everyone is a sports fan. Rank and title have no place there. The game is everything. Watching the ball is all that matters.

Keeping faith

The most difficult thing for any sports club to achieve is to keep faith with all of its fans, all the year round. If the club is successful, and has a large following, it is impossible for the management to know the name and address of every supporter unless they have a comprehensive computerized ticket system. Very few sports clubs have considered that this is necessary, because they have too many fans to fill the available seats. They ask 'Why should we spend a lot of money on computerized ticketing, when the fans are fighting to buy them.'

In my many conversations with ticket managers, in many parts of the world, I can see a trend away from stadium attendance. The television broadcasts are making more and more people stay at home. The violence in the stands is another contributing factor, as we have seen. But if the bad behaviour can be reduced to a minimum, as everyone thinks it can be, then the sports staffs are left with the sole problem of continuing to attract the families, despite TV broadcasts. My proposal has been the same to them all, 'How did the Readers Digest organization overcome the problem of falling sales? The answer is the same! Buy a computer. Put all of your supporters' names and addresses into the computer's memory. Make each entrance into the ground just as automized as a supermarket check-out. Then, you will know who comes, how often, where they live, where they sit, and how much they are willing to pay for a seat. Then, when the special big matches come along, the allocation of tickets at Wembley (or wherever) is not only easy, but it will be fair. Gone will be the days of supporters grumbling that they come every week but are forgotten at the Cup Finals. And, gone will be the days of the all-night queues for any spare tickets.'

Keeping faith with the fans, all the year round, is not easy – even in the supporters' clubs – never mind just at the big matches. This means looking after every detail of each supporter's needs. One day, I challenged the senior staff about the quality of the food which was then available in the club snack bars on match days. I had run a test on it, and felt that if Egon Ronay had been with me, Tottenham Hotspur would have had a special 'consolation prize' in his restaurant ratings. I was amazed to discover that none of the senior staff had even thought of trying it for themselves. They had not done their own independent assessment. They had their separate bars and tea rooms, which they knew served good food. If the chaplain is the only person who is fully aware of what is happening to the fans, and how they are being treated and catered for, then he must be permitted to have a voice where it counts. He is a vital link in the chain which leads to success in the future, if the TV broadcasts are not to win. Whatever else happens in sport, the fans must be encouraged!

11: Links With The Past

Every football club programme is interesting to read, because of the way that the management approach the subject. As a writer, I have found it fascinating to buy programmes wherever possible at away-matches, in order to make comparisons between the various clubs. Overseas clubs have such a different approach from anything in Britain, because of the differences of culture and race between us all. We have a lot to learn from each other.

Good club programmes

One feature in the Spurs programmes which always interests me is the 'What Happened to Them?' concerning previous players. On a regular basis, we can read about the present health, prosperity, job, and whereabouts of those stars of yesterday whom we used to cheer and applaud. Men like Martin Chilvers, Arthur Rowe, Roger Morgan, Cyril Knowles, and Alfie Conn have all had a vital part to play in the success of the Tottenham Hotspur Club, and it is only right that we should all be made to remember them and be aware of their present situation.

I think that it was in 1979 that the programme ran a story about Maurice Norman in this 'What Happened to Them?' column. From memory, we were told that Maurice had a leg broken in a match at White Hart Lane, just before Christmas in 1965, and that he now lives in Frinton-on-Sea in Essex where he and his wife Jacqueline have a wool shop on Connaught Avenue.

Since then, I have been intending to visit that wool shop the next time that I find myself in Frinton-on-Sea! So far, I haven't achieved it, but in view of all that Maurice contributed to the Spurs, I owe him such a visit. Maurice was the Spurs centre-half in the great season of 1960–61, and was at Tottenham for 10 good years. During his time at White Hart Lane, he made over 20 appearances for England, as well as helping the Spurs to achieve victory at Wembley and in Europe. It is right that such players are remembered.

I was pleased that I was associated with a club which did have the right kind of respect about its previous players. In my own small way, I have tried to do the same about the Christian sportsmen of the past, in order that the present church-going young people do not forget. In my six-monthly Letter for Prayer about my work at Tottenham, which was circulated worldwide, I mentioned one of these 'men from the past' each time.

From Ipswich to India

At the height of his career with Ipswich Town, Bert Haste scored as many as 53 goals in a season. In his last match there, he put the ball into the net four times! Bert was an excellent footballer. In 1926, he left all that behind to go to Bible College in order to become a missionary. In 1928, he set off for India, where he served faithfully for 18 years, before returning to England where he took charge of a church in a small village. That's where he was when I first met him, and how patient and zealous he seemed to me to be. Bert went to Weymouth to live in his retirement, and it was from Weymouth that Graham Roberts came as a young man to the Spurs. One day, I asked Graham if he knew Bert Haste, and if–in Weymouth–they looked after this remarkable footballer from the past. Graham had never heard of him, but promised to look him up on a visit. I have travelled to India, to see where Bert Haste spent those 18 long years, and I have stood on the steps of the Cornhill in Ipswich, where Bert used to speak to passers-by about his Lord, on a Sunday evening, after having run himself into the ground at Portman Road the previous day. These links with the past are helpful for all Christians in sport.

From Yugoslavia with love

The 1936 Olympic Games are now remembered mainly because of the frequent appearances of the great non-runner

Adolf Hitler. In Berlin that year, politics dominated the stadium, even though some famous athletes did well. The following war years encouraged the stories which had been circulated in the Olympic changing rooms, and notable achievements were forgotten in the light of the bravery on the military fields. However, there were some who not only shone in Berlin in 1936, but also gained high honours in battle, and survived until recently as true heroes.

One such man was Alexander Kovacevic. As a lad in Yugoslavia before the Second World War, he had been the idol of the girls, with his tall and straight figure, blond hair, smiling features, and handsome appearances. Known to the royal family, as well as to the common man, Alex was a national hero, and a well-loved sportsman.

In Berlin, he did not achieve a gold medal, although that had been expected, because he found the political pressures there too distracting. Nevertheless, in other world events, he attracted honours and titles, which ensured his lasting fame as a Yugoslav athlete of the highest stature.

In 1939, the sun stopped shining in his country because the Nazis looked upon Yugoslavia as a likely area into which they could easily expand. Alex enlisted under the flag of General Mihailovich in 1941, when King Peter sought to oppose both the Nazis and the Russians (who at that time were allies of Hitler), in a bold attempt to rid the country of both fascist and communistic elements. The plan failed when the Germans suddenly changed their tactics and invaded Russia, thus putting King Peter and General Mihailovich against the Allies (who had now been joined by Russia).

As a guerilla soldier in the mountains, never sure who (or where) the enemy was (now that the communists had their own pro-Russian leader in General Tito), Alex became a confused nationalist. The Western Allies had encouraged the Chetniks (the Mihailovich guerillas) in the beginning, but now – through pressure from Moscow – they stopped sending all supplies. In such a situation, this lovable athlete wondered if the Christian faith meant the same to Winston Churchill as it did to him, or was there the possibility of compromise with those who were out to destroy freedom in the land he so personally loved? The execution of Mihailovich by Tito, for treason, was the last straw for Alex Kovacevic. He left

Yugoslavia with secret help and escaped to England, where he arrived penniless. Taking any job he could find, he melted into the background of the London scene and could be recognized only because of his height and fine features. When he walked into my church one Sunday, he was instantly recognizable to those who had any love for Yugoslavia, and together we rediscovered the joy of love for a country, despite everything.

Before he died, in 1979, Alex had helped to train other sportspeople, including Mary Rand, and had shared his glowing faith with thousands. His hug on a Sunday morning is now only a memory, but such a link with the past, through such a noble sports personality, is a bonus that the people of Wood Green and Tottenham cannot forget.

To Durban from Bristol

When J. F. Rowlands arrived in Durban, South Africa, he knew only that he had to speak to the Indians about the Lord Jesus. Nothing else was clear to him. He had been happy to play football for Bristol, but the divine call to give this up and to go to South Africa in order to preach the Gospel to the Indians was too real to ignore. When he had that divine guidance, he did not know that there were any Indians in Africa, but a visit to an expert quickly assured him that there were a lot in the Durban area.

By renting a shop, and using it as a base from which to work, J. F. Rowlands set out to commence one of the fastest-growing churches in the world. Since 1932, so much has been achieved that it reads like something out of the Acts of the Apostles. The Bethesda Centre in Carlisle Street, Durban, is a monument to one footballer who could not stay on the field, and who finally had to hang up his boots in the service of God.

One of his early converts told me, before she died, that 'J.F.' used to illustrate some of his sermons in those initial days with stories about football in Britain. She never did understand what he was talking about until she came to live in Tottenham. There, seeing the huge crowds making their way to the White Hart Lane ground, she began to appreciate the tales she had heard years before. Such links with the past are like history in action, and we shall never be able to understand the future, if we dare not face up to the lessons of yesterday.

12: Putting Religion In Its Place

For any sporting club, the main problem with having a chaplain around is that he is religious! Anyone who has been into a rugby football changing room will know that sportsmen can be *very* irreligious! Within minutes of my arrival at White Hart Lane, Pat Welton took me on one side and said that he could not guarantee that I would not hear swearing. When I explained that bad language was pretty common in North London, and had been in the engineering circles in which I had moved, he was clearly relieved. In fact, I heard very little swearing, but it is possible that everyone was restrained when I was around!

Do sport and religion mix?

The film *Chariots of Fire* received lots of praise and not a few Hollywood Oscar awards. If religion and sport do not mix, and if cinema audiences are too sophisticated for religious movies, why did this film do so well?

For the well-read sportsman, this was not a new story. Eric Liddell had been deeply interested in both the Christian faith and athletics, but always concluded that worship must come before any self-interest. There was nothing strange in this for those who have been brought up in evangelical congregations, where it is believed that one does not dash out of morning worship in order to drive out to the beach or the golf club. Perhaps those who hold such views today are the minority group in church-attending people, but Eric's problem is not a novel one for millions of Christians all over the world today.

His story was published in little booklets by Scottish tract societies, and handed out by eager Sunday School teachers, years ago. It is a tale that many of us have grown up with, alongside those concerning William Carey, David Livingstone, Mary Slessor, C. T. Studd, and Gladys Aylward. For us, the challenge was not so much that religion and sport do not mix, but that sport on Sunday causes compromise. In his wisdom, David Puttnam decided that the challenge of such a compromise could (if properly presented) attract crowds of cinema-goers.

There is little doubt that Eric Liddell was a hero to the lads of his own generation, but it may come as a bit of a shock to some that he can be a hero for large numbers of non-church-going people today.

The success of this film (and that of the *Inn of the Sixth Happiness*, and others like them) proves that stories of those who have lived noble lives and have maintained standards against the tide of human behaviour, are still wanted. Some may sneer, but the majority applaud true bravery and warm to uplifting sentiments. And, football fans are no different from the rest!

Going too far

The young zealot is always anxious to do everything instantly, and take everything to its limit without delay. For this reason, the young chaplains are not as patient as I have been, and want to see quicker results than those I was able to obtain. As I explained in the opening chapter, my role developed slowly, over two years. I did nothing in a hurry, and made changes very slowly. For this, I have been criticized by those on the outside. The folk at White Hart Lane never wanted me to hurry anyway, and so my unwillingness to make haste was not faulted by them.

As I see things, each sporting club is different because of the role it plays in its community, because of its commercial situation, and because of the attitude of its management. For this reason, one would approach each club differently. If a new chaplain was appointed to a sporting club composed of all Christian athletes, he would have a completely different situation from the one into which I was introduced, and could start at a different level. On the other hand, if a new chaplain was appointed to a sporting club in which there was no interest at all, and the management was opposed to the appointment, he would also have a completely different situation from the one that I had to face. We all have to start from where we begin.

The furthest that I went in praying publicly, was before a meal when many were present; sermonizing was limited to short bursts in private; and quoting the Bible dogmatically was never done, except when requested. I set out with the idea that I would introduce the Christian faith only if appropriate, and would make my main ministry that of being a benevolent influence. Some would see this as a low target at which to aim. Those who know what life is like in First Division British football might consider that I was not too far wrong. The big question is, did I succeed, at all? Ossie Ardiles is on record as having said, 'It is the benevolent calm which surrounds David that I value most. I am aware of that before and during every home match. I only wish that he could be with us, in the same way, at every away-match as well.'

Christians in sport

There have been committed Christians in competitive sports since the days of St Paul, and there have been famous ones for hundreds of years. During the past two centuries, some eminent sportspeople have become leaders in the Christian Church. One cannot separate men like C. T. Studd and Eric Liddell from David Sheppard, just because one is still alive. Such people form a glorious team that is timeless.

In the same way, Chackop Jacob and Sekhur Mondal working in their own ways amongst sportspeople in India are no different from the spectacular all-Christian basketball teams in North America, even though they don't appear on television and get their names in the national papers. The little-known Christians who are plodding on with the task of seeking to be a beneficial influence on sport are no less important than those American Christian sportsmen who have their own radio shows in the USA.

First of all in America, and then in Europe, sporting Christians began to get together and form themselves into national groups. Organizations such as 'Athletes in Action' have now been triplicated in their own country, and others (like the British 'Christians in Sport') are being copied on other continents. The aim is fellowship and encouragement for those who are often alone in their own team or sport. At the international level, and especially at the Olympic Games, these new inter-church sports groups really come into their own, providing links across the national barriers and giving support where needed.

For the chaplain in sport, these organizations are a lifeline, binding everyone together. It was because I had heard of Dave Merrington and seen his name on a list, that I looked out for him as the Leeds team began to climb back on to their coach after a game at White Hart Lane. As soon as I introduced myself, his arms went out in a spontaneous welcome. Those who had heard of each other had now met! It has been the same with others, all over the world.

Trips overseas

Some international sports teams get to travel a lot these days, giving some of their spare time to short tours and special one-night-stand matches. Everywhere that teams travel, they leave behind an abiding impression. Whenever they set off, I stayed home and worried about the safety of the Spurs lads, and wondered what the local people would think of them. A lot of prayer went up each time they flew off!

At the big matches in Britain, I was more anxious about the behaviour of the fans, or – after the Wembley wins – that of the apprentices who drank too much. However, in all of these situations, I was never let down. As they left on one trip some of the lads actually promised (after I had intimated that friends of mine out there were going to be at the match), 'Don't worry Dave; we won't spoil your image.'

In fact, whenever the Spurs team appeared in public, they were much smarter than many a modern businessman, and behaved so well that one could only praise them. Most of the awards for this must go to the fine example of the Tottenham management whilst I was there. Keith Burkinshaw had a Yorkshire Methodist upbringing, which affects all of his attitudes regarding behaviour, and Peter

Shreeves spent many happy years in the Boys Brigade. These influences were always obvious to any thinking observer.

Cliff Richard

Some years ago, I was given the job of asking Cliff Richard if he would consider giving some of his time, without payment, to the cause of seeking to influence British sportspeople with the Christian faith. My daughter Ruth and I approached him with some diffidence because he was already busy and so many others had made similar requests. I took Ruth with me because she is a fan of Cliff as well as of the Spurs. In a committee, as we considered this, again and again Cliff seemed to be the right person. He has the sort of personality that appeals to sportspeople, and his music appeals to many. It is thrilling that he agreed to do this, whenever his timetable permits. Already, he has been a great influence on many. I have seen him hold the attention of soccer players for over an hour, when others could not have kept them listening for more than five minutes. But, none of this was in Spurs time; it was on the day-off, after hours, in private gatherings. And, only those who volunteered to attend came along – none were pressurized into attending.

Meeting other Christians

One thing which made the Spurs appointment a pleasure for me was the constant round of meeting interesting people. By being in the right place at the right time, it was possible to chat with the stars of stage and screen, and most of the football players from the past. By the door into the 'tunnel', one could see as much as the commissionaire at a film première. Some of the chats I had with such people provided me with a flow of illustrations for preaching that will last for a long time!

However, the most rewarding of those meetings were with the Christian soccer players, because the conversation changed immediately if they passed by. Richard Powling, Justin Fashanu, Mervyn Cawston, Alan West, Ian Bolton, and Mark Kendall are just a few that I have chatted with at one ground or another, and all of them have given me a new look on life. Their enthusiasm has helped me, and given me fresh encouragement to continue patiently.

If I had been involved in cricket, I would have met more of the David Sheppard's of this world, and (amongst the ladies) more like Jill Powell. However, my eyesight did not permit me to see a fast-moving ball sufficiently well to play that game. Equally, if I had heeded my father's advice and taken up golf when I was younger, I may have got to know people like Larry Nelson. By the same argument, I might have met George Foreman if I had been a boxer, Stan Smith and Margaret Court if I had been a tennis player (I have met Sue Barker!), and Rudy Hartono if I had been anything more than an amateur at badminton. These are well-known Christians who have been successful in sport, and they attract our admiration. Their success, and their clear testimony, make the work of all chaplains that much easier.

Fun with our faith

Whilst other newspapers were finding reasons to fault me, or misquoting me, some went out of their way to help. One even did a cover that I cherish. The little-known *Maintenance and Equipment News* magazine carried a cartoon on its cover for one of its editions, by Gordon Stowell. This depicted a church that had been covered in graffiti heralding 'Spurs for the Cup!', and a clergyman walking away from it who himself was also covered in similar graffiti but which included 'Blessed are the Peacemakers'.

The shouts of 'Said your prayers today?' and 'Watch out, here's the bloody parson!' were never said in anger. They were just as much bursts of fun as the constant 'Shoot the ref!' Everyone knew that I had a job to do, and by applying humour, we all coped very well.

13: Praise And Encouragement

The manager was very clear in his advice and assessment of what I had been asked to undertake. On the first day, he took me through into the dressing room to meet the lads, saying that he did not expect me to make any progress at all for at least a year. Then, after I had been introduced, he suggested that I might discover that one of the most helpful things that I could attempt would be to encourage those who were disappointed or had just been disciplined.

It is a rare manager who can be everything to everyone, all of the time. If a player has to be punished, the scar can heal quickly or slowly, depending on the tactics used. Instant forgiveness on both sides is not common in soccer. Perhaps the players are more easily able to forgive and forget than the staff, because they do not have the long-term prosperity of the club as a *permanent* responsibility. When the manager sees a game lost, a penalty forfeited, or fans distressed, he has more on his mind than the immediate problem; he can see years of hard work being lost on account of the behaviour of just one undisciplined lad, and he (understandably) is not very happy.

Every general, factory manager, shopkeeper, and clergyman has known the temptation to throw his anger at the offender and then remain bitter for weeks. At one time, such offenders would lose their jobs if not their heads. Today, we are more tolerant, but human feelings cannot be erased just because the law is now not so tough as once it was.

On hand to help

When I was a student apprentice, learning the engineering profession on the factory floor, I was present when one of the men made a mistake which cost the company thousands of pounds. In 1946, this was a large sum, and he was dismissed instantly. Despite my youth, I approached the management about this man, and pleaded for him to retain his job, in view of his age, his commitments, and his family. I obtained no concessions, and the man gathered up his tools and walked out of the gates. Having failed in one direction, I now sought references for him from his fellow-workers, and then went to his home and advised him about jobs that were on offer in other factories that I had approached on his behalf. Within a week, he was employed again.

Considering that I was only 18 years old at the time, this was no small feat. However, I never will understand sport as well as I then understood my own original profession. For that reason, there was never any hope that I could assist footballers who needed a transfer. In any case, British soccer is a complicated world in which managers, agents and players are the only ones who really know what is happening.

During the many years of pastoral care, I have learned all the lessons that one has to learn if somebody dies, is ill, discovers that his wife has left him, loses his job, finds out that his son is on drugs, wants to get married, and so on. There are right ways and wrong ways to approach people in all circumstances. Then, having learned all these things, one has to learn how to use that information with those who have this and that kind of personality. Being a counsellor has never been easy.

Some have given years of their lives in order to be good counsellors. Appreciating all the twists and turns of human nature, and knowing when to speak and when to be silent is a profession in itself these days. Such experts are valuable in politics, the armed services, industry, and colleges. And, as every teacher knows, they are no less important in schools. Why do people behave in the way that they do, and is it possible to show them the faults in their characters sufficiently to enable them to make less mistakes in the future?

I found that football players have problems that I had not met before and get themselves into situations that are not found in other professions. Within a few weeks, I realized that I was in another world, about which very few outside the sport know anything. It took me a long time to see life from a player's point of view, and even longer to appreciate all the pressures upon the staff. A football manager's take-home worries are neither less nor more than those of an industrial chief, but his sudden shocks are worse. And, considering that the fortunes of his club may depend upon the attitudes of a dozen young lads, sleepless nights can be much more common. A young chaplain might appear to be a good choice, in view of the ages of the majority involved, but the experience of an older one would be more useful in the long run.

Appreciating everyone

If I had been the chaplain of the Boston Bruins at that never-to-be-forgotten game when almost the whole of their hockey team invaded a stand and attacked some of the people in the crowd with their hockey sticks, I may have found it difficult to praise them afterwards! If nothing else, I would have wanted to have understood what caused such a backlash and to have asked them if they did not – at any point during this extensive clash – think of the effect that their behaviour would have on the game. The interesting thing about human behaviour is that when our minds are full of anger, we don't think about the effect of our actions on others. During the heat of those moments, *others* have to tell us not to forget the neighbours (or whoever is most affected). The emotion blots out all concern for others. A chaplain has the task of trying to make everyone see that the rest *do matter*, and that nobody is too insignificant to be overlooked.

At big British soccer matches, the police are a vital factor in the successful running of each event. Without them, there may be confusion and chaos. The public is aware of this, but one would have to go inside a football club, and be close to those who work with the police, in order to discover that the police on duty will feel more appreciated if their needs are remembered, and if such a small courtesy as making sure that each one gets a copy of the programme is not forgotten.

Each person present is just as important as the others, as far as he is concerned, and it takes careful organization to ensure that nobody feels neglected. From the youngest fan to the richest supporter, from the gateman to the chairman of the board of directors, and from the latest schoolboy-signing to the longest-serving professional, all have a vital role to play. To keep them all happy, and to ensure that they all feel appreciated is a big undertaking that crosses so many human barriers and emotional dividing lines. Being the manager of a factory can be easier than being the manager of a large sporting club, even though more are in the factory each working day.

'Mighty citadel'

Michael Hart of the London *Standard* has described the club that I have been associated with as a 'mighty citadel of the game'. Clearly, he meant that it is one of the most important soccer clubs in the world. It is a privilege for anyone to be associated with such a club. The young lads joining as apprentices are aware of this, even as every special visitor is. The awful failing in most of us is that we easily forget our privileges. Familiarity breeds contempt, even in the most thinking person.

Too quickly, the apprentice becomes a professional, plays before a crowd, is seen by another club, and is in demand. With similar speed, the notion that it is a privilege to be involved with a leading club is forgotten. As soon as that idea leaves the mind, the sense of appreciation becomes like a foreign body – it is not needed, and so is cast aside. When a young player decides that he no longer needs instruction, it is difficult to reach him, and all approaches may fail. He now does not need encouragement or praise; he needs to see that personal success relies upon the success of one's team, and that without total commitment to that team his success may vanish as mist.

Too many of those who visit Portugal fly straight to the South in order to catch as much of the sun as possible, and so miss the capital Lisbon. As all football supporters know, Lisbon is the home of the Benfica club. Any stay in Lisbon is not complete without a visit to the trophy room of this (another) citadel of soccer. The cups and awards are both huge and numerous. Their size and quantity overwhelm the tourist.

However, all these trophies (like those in every other major sporting club) are the result of total team commitment, month in and month out, for year after year, regardless of the attraction of money, and in spite of the rebelliousness which can affect the few. Unfortunately, such trophies are not all that some sportsmen are concerned about now.

Personal problems

An eminent politician has suggested that ten years can be a long time. Certainly, many changes can be seen in each sports club in ten years. In that time, a player-captain of a small local club (such as Ron Atkinson) can become the manager of a famous national club (in this case, Manchester United). In those few years, each team can change completely and both the manager and the chairman of the directors may be replaced. The continuing club may only be recognizable by its office and ground staff. The changes can be so sudden, and so overwhelming that the fans may wonder who they will see on the pitch next Saturday, or who will be in charge next week.

Such uncertainty affects everybody else who is, even remotely, connected with the club, and it can have devastating effects. When a team is already facing frustration because of its passing inability to win points, the added aggravation of not knowing who the next manager will be, or which players will be playing tomorrow, is no help.

If, on top of that, a player has a personal problem, life may appear (even temporarily) to be caving in. A sick wife or daughter can be the last straw if there are other dominant frustrations. An unkind newspaper report, just at the wrong time, is equally distressing, and a claim for damages through an injury on the field (which is the new phantom for sports people) can break the spirit of the most hardened player.

Praise and encouragement are well-tried medicines in the midst of such conflicts and confusions, but if they are applied in the wrong way and in the wrong amounts (and particularly at the wrong times) even this remedy can fail. Some people don't want praise, even when they need it, and to force it on them can do harm. Others only want encouragement from those from whom they choose to receive it. Understanding differences, and meeting the need for praise and encouragement just when they are required, is not easy to learn. Mistakes are made here even by the most talented experts. A chaplain has the advantage of knowing he can pray before he speaks to people and so ought to make less errors in this field of human counselling than most. Nevertheless, what he does and says can still be criticized, and frequently is. Like the players, a chaplain can have a bad day and make mistakes. If he does, he needs just as much praise and encouragement as the next person!

14: Christmas, And The Festive Seasons

One of my most unforgettable memories is connected with the Tottenham Hotspur Football Club one Christmas. For someone who has travelled widely, and lived for more than half a century, this can only mean that the event was special.

It was almost Christmas Eve, and the club had arranged a party for the children of the players and staff. The entertainment and the food were of the highest quality, and everyone was in a festive mood. It had been a happy season so far, and there was an atmosphere of hope and expectancy about the place. Even the unmarried players came in to enjoy the fun, realizing that this was to be a special time for the children, and the more who were there the happier everyone would be.

It was already dark outside, and the seasonal lighting on the High Road tempted one to forget that this was downtown Tottenham; the gaiety within and the colour outside brought to all of our minds the happy Christmases that we had known when we were all little children.

Suddenly (although it was organized, in fact), someone said, 'It must be time for Father Christmas!' We were all encouraged to go and stand by the windows, and watch for the arrival of the expected winter visitor. Just as we put our noses to the glass, snow began to fall! This had not been arranged, but it was remarkably efficient in its timing! Then, with snowflakes descending in ever-increasing quantity, a larger-than-life Santa Claus came into the car park, opposite the windows, in a little pony cart, loaded down with sacks of presents.

The pony drew him ever nearer to the window, and I looked along to see the effect on everyone. Just near me were Sylvia Ardiles and her children; their faces were a picture;

they were entranced by the scene! Too soon, the magic disappeared! Santa Claus was actually Jimmy Holmes, and although he made a magnificent job of it, by coming inside the poetry faded. The children loved the presents, the players were grateful for the generosity shown, the wives were pleased to be so well-cared-for, and everyone was happy.

As for me, I shall not forget the expressions on those little Argentinian faces, as an exuberant Father Christmas came in through the snow!

Making the most

Everyone expects pastors to make the most of Christmas, and to take a religious opportunity when it is possible. Even if chaplains (of every variety) do not overdo the religious factor during the rest of the year, we excuse them if they take the initiative at Christmas, Easter and Whitsuntide. I had heard of chaplains who led carol-concerts in prisons, who organized carol-singing on the wards in hospitals, and who arranged camp-concerts in barracks in the Army, but knew nothing of anything similar in sports clubs.

The idea of drumming up support for some carol-singing in place of canned music before the Christmas match, did fleet momentarily through my mind, but wasn't encouraged. There were other ideas that were no more exciting and much less sensible, until I came to the notion that someone like me could make Christmas into a season for visiting.

Visiting the players of any major football club is never easy because they tend to live miles apart. If the club is based on a county town, and the training ground is on the right side, at least everyone can be reached without crossing the town centre. As far as London is concerned, the players live like scattered sparks on a catherine wheel, and so calling on them all in one week becomes well-nigh impossible. In any case, as we all know, churches are most busy at the festive seasons and so one cannot spend too much time driving around visiting footballers in the hope that they might be at home.

The first Christmas, I managed only two such visits, and they were only partly successful. Mark Kendall then lived in a flat within walking distance of the club. His wife worked in the commercial office at the ground. By planning carefully, I was able to make sure that Mark and his wife would be at home if I called on them at the right time. This was my first such visit and I loved it. Going into a home and sharing something of the warmth and affection of Christmas with its occupants was a real joy.

A day later, I walked past Peter Taylor's shop at Westcliff, in order to look through the door and see if he was inside. If I had judged it right, he ought to be there, but I couldn't see him. As I turned round to come back and look again, Peter bounded out towards me and welcomed me like a long-lost cousin, so that – instead of me paying him a visit – he dragged me inside!

The following Christmases saw me trudging up to other doors, and making better friendships on this informal level, in the happy season.

Easter, and all that

More lively chaplains will be much more fruitful in their relationships with other teams than I have been able to achieve, and they will think up better ways of making Christmas, Easter and Whitsuntide come alive to those they minister to. In between all the rush of the pre-match activity at these special times, British clubs find it difficult to do too much, for fear of over-tiring players who must rest in preparation for the next game. However, if personal conversations can spread the message of the seasons, with or without any special activity, a sports chaplain will be achieving more than many had dreamt might be possible only a few years ago.

15: Getting The Basis Right

Modern sport is organized and team sports are more organized than any other. As a result when anyone enters them, he or she must be aware of all the pitfalls before going too far. A sports chaplain is no different from any other, except that – at the time of writing – there is not yet any basis laid down for him. He is given no rules or guidelines and he signs no contract, apart from the North American clubs where they are blazing a trail.

When a pastor becomes a hospital chaplain, he becomes an employee of the hospital or the Area Health Authority. Their rules and conditions are binding upon him. The same is true in the prison service, the armed services, colleges of further education, teacher-training colleges, and mental institutions. Every employee in these professions has a set of rules given to him or her, and a contract is signed.

The need for a contract

In every profession, a chaplain can easily obtain access to information of a confidential nature. If it is hospital, by studying the admissions lists, he could discover that a famous film star is in a room having an operation of a sensitive kind. If he is not bound to a contract, he might (if he was that sort of a person) sell this information to the tabloid daily newspapers.

In the same way, a chaplain in the armed services could divulge matters of a secret nature which might help an enemy, if he had not committed himself to secrecy. When he took up the task of being a chaplain to soldiers, sailors and airmen, he also – at the same time – vowed never to break the code of confidentiality. In all professions, it is the same: the signing chaplain knows what he is committing himself to, what limits are imposed upon him, and what is permitted.

Because, to date, sports chaplains have been appointed without contracts none have been sure of the guidelines and everyone is learning by his mistakes.

Should chaplains be paid?

One of the reasons why there are very few contracts in sport for chaplains is because sports clubs have not seen the need. They assume that men in pastoral office are completely trustworthy and so contracts are not necessary. Another reason is because the majority of sports chaplains are not paid and a contract is usually only necessary if there is some payment.

When I was asked to take up this work, I stipulated that I must *not* be paid. Upon reflection, I can see that this was a mistake because I then did not have the assistance of a contract, and could be described as 'not being on the staff' if anyone wished to exclude me from something. My reason for being so definite was simple: I did not want any of the players to think that I was doing it because I was paid to do it. I thought then that I could not open up new avenues of this sort if, in their minds, there was even the suspicion of a thought that I would not be there if it was not for the cash I was being paid.

It is possible that I was naïve at this point, and that I should have asked for a small payment and a contract. Certainly, with hindsight, I would advise all other budding chaplains in sport to insist on this. My concern now would not be connected with the cash but with the need to have a job in the organization – and so be recognized. It does not matter if everyone else on the staff knows that the chaplain puts in all these hours and gets only peanuts for doing it. It does matter that he is a part-time employee, and has a recognized task in the club.

Perhaps one day, when the value of sports chaplains has been recognized, the situation can be improved internationally. Then, along with other vital members of the club staff, the chaplain will not only be paid and have a contract, but he will be employed full-time. This will ensure that he is always on hand, and that his services are available at every training session and every home and away-match.

To each his corner

In every profession and in every trade, each employee has his own special place that can be called his own. It may be a very humble bench or desk, and he may have to share it with another, but – somewhere in that factory, office, hospital, farm, or army – each has a corner which is his or her own.

As one who has worked on a factory floor, and mixed with the most ordinary workers all over the world, I know that everyone needs somewhere to hang his clothes and put his tools. It may be a very humble corner that some workers have, and in a very simple workshop, but it is there, and every other worker in that place is aware of who puts his tools and coat where.

A sports chaplain needs such a spot, in order to have a base from which to work. If he is going to train with the lads, then he will be allocated a locker. If that is not possible, then he must be allocated something else instead, so that – if nothing else – he has a hook that is his own, whilst he is there.

When someone wants to find him, they ought to know where to look. If one of the players or member of staff wants a private chat, there should be somewhere that the conversation can be held. To ask for an office in a Third Division sports club is unrealistic, but a room or an office that is used only on Saturdays could be set aside during the week. Embarrassed lads like to feel that their words are not overheard, and walls are the only way to stop curious ears from listening.

Time to work

When I began this intriguing work, I was already working a seven-day week and lacking proper holidays. To give up a Friday morning and a Saturday afternoon was like making a Churchillian sacrifice. I still don't know how I did it, but I remember that my wife was not pleased! As a full-time teacher, she had always hoped that we could have a little part of Saturday together, but chaplaincy work in sport meant that this was impossible. For us, the other six days of every week were already sacrificed for other things.

As time passed, the role demanded more and more time,

and so – finally – the whole of Saturday was surrendered, as well as two mornings, Friday afternoons, and most Wednesday evenings. This is a large part of any pastor's week and it would mean for most that there was then no hope of a day off. Also, in my case, because my wife's fixed holidays did not harmonize with the football summer break, it meant that we were not able to have a proper holiday together.

This kind of sacrifice is easier if the chaplain is older and his family doesn't mind. In some clubs I have visited, the strain put upon part-time chaplains was so great that his own marriage began to collapse. This is why a full-time post would be better. This way, everyone has leisure time on the same days, and holidays can be linked with the absence of the team from the ground.

In order that conversations can have time, and in order that there are plenty of opportunities for counselling of every kind, for the First Team, their families, the staff, and the fans, sports chaplaincy cannot be a ministry which is confined to a few hours each week. This must be understood by everyone involved from the very beginning. A timetable must be agreed, and duties understood.

Areas of responsibility

Because of the sort of people that they are, and the education that they have had, pastors are expected to be able to do almost anything at a moment's notice. I suddenly found myself entertaining a group of Norwegian soccer coaches, welcoming the directors of a Spanish club, making light conversation with film stars, solving the ticket problems of visiting managers, explaining the game to an American tennis player, calming down fans who had been double-booked in seats, explaining to an irate visitor why he could not park his car in the car park, and occupying the attention of an important supporter for long enough so that by the time he took his seat he would not know that there had been some difficulties.

Usually, there are others to attend to these things, and they do them very well. Most major clubs have everything worked out very carefully. However, those people have emergencies of their own sometimes, and then a further pair of hands is required. I found myself coming in useful, in all sorts of ways, because I was trusted to be diplomatic, friendly, faithful, and trustworthy. The same can be said of every chaplain in every professional situation.

However, by doing this kind of thing, and filling-in for others, it is easy to be taken away from one's own area of responsibility, and then questions are asked as to why you are not in your place at the right time. Pleasing everyone is never easy and that is why there must always be clear lines of authority in every organization. The chaplain must know to whom he is responsible and whose orders he should regard as being authoritative. In a crisis situation, with the staff under pressure, it is imperative that each knows his own area of responsibility and ensures that this role is completely fulfilled.

The place of religion

In the sports clubs which are wholly Hindu, with everyone in it being of that same faith and speaking the same language, the appointed chaplain will expect that he will be permitted to have a clear religious role within the membership. The same is true in a soccer team in a Moslem country; there, the chaplain would know that most of the players and staff would have united views about times of prayer and days for worship.

In the West, things are not so clearcut, and each club has its own view on things. With the religious climate as it is, each manager and chaplain has to find his own way, and decide upon a balance. This is because so many clubs are in multi-religious communities and no one religion is accepted by everybody. For that reason, there has to be an agreement that religion will go only so far, and that any conversations about religion will be held only at the request of the enquirer. This does not mean that a chaplain must compromise his own faith, but that he must adjust his activity to the environment he is in. His situation is no different from that of a missionary in a multi-cultural city. He must tread carefully and use wisdom in his approaches.

In some countries, a club might be composed only of

people who adhere firmly to the Roman Catholic faith. In others, a similar club might embrace totally the faith of the Protestant reformers. The situation changes from club to club, and country to country. The guidelines must be associated with the sports club alone, and cannot be decided nationally, unless there is a national religion.

Knowing and being known

Walking along a street in downtown Buffalo, which lies on the southern bank of Lake Erie in the American state of New York, I decided upon a little test. Were all of these city people on the side-walk aware of their local football club, did they know the name of its manager, and did they know if it had a chaplain?

Reaching the Greyhound Bus Station, I began my survey, thinking that, here, the people would have time to talk. Making sure, first of all, that I was chatting with genuine Buffalo residents and not tourists, I popped my questions.

Without any hesitation all of the men knew names, and one could even give me the chaplain's address! This was all so different from the situation in most of the rest of the world. In Liverpool, the average fan would not know if the club had a chaplain; in Milan he would not care, and in Calcutta it would not matter. In so many American towns and cities, the chaplain is known and appreciated. Does this mean that clubs in other countries are too shy to make their appointments known? Or, are they afraid to let the world know that they are giving religion a foothold in their organization? Perhaps, it is just that American people are very open about all that they do, and there is little secrecy in their communities.

Clearly, there is an advantage in everyone knowing that a pastor is available, that he has been properly appointed, and that his name is to be found in the handbook or programme. Such publicity will make life much easier for everyone, and it will stop information spreading just by word of mouth – which can be so unreliable. Obviously, the role of the chaplain must not be elevated so high that people think that he is a very important part of the administration, but it is important to his task that everyone knows his name, knows where to contact him, and which days he will be on hand.

Humour with everything

Being with sportspeople can be very humorous indeed and their company is rarely depressing. However, the fans are no less humorous in their own way.

When the Spurs are playing on a Wednesday evening, the whole area is cluttered with cars and so movement before and after the matches can be difficult. The fans arriving mingle with the workers going home and the local young people going out to attend some other social function. On top of all this, there is the normal flow of traffic in both directions, up and down the High Road.

In order to be there early enough to see all the players arrive, I walked to the ground, taking all the possible short-cuts, down the side streets. Then, after I had seen all the players and staff go into the dressing-room and watched the opposing side arrive, I went back to my church because its regular mid-week meeting is held on a Wednesday evening.

In order to be at the church on time, I had to run along the Lordship Lane, because there was no hope of a bus with all that traffic. Seeing me running away from White Hart Lane, the fans who were now pouring along the streets in the direction of the ground thought up all kinds of humorous remarks to make, to me and about me. To them it seemed that if the chaplain was running away things must be pretty awful! Over the years, the regulars got to the place where they would expect me and had thought up all kinds of funny things to say, just as we crossed paths.

After the match, and at the right time, my wife would drive me in her car as near to the ground as possible, drop me off, and then try to get back home before the traffic made *that* impossible. Now, the same fans would see me running *towards* the ground, as if I was late for the game, or anxious to be there! If the Spurs had lost, their cat-calls were in strong language, and they gave me all kinds of advice about what to say to which of the players!

Wednesday evenings are much less strenuous these days,

but they are not the same! If there is one thing that I miss now, it is that flow of punchlines from the advancing fans, as I ran towards them. It was a genial (though often cutting) humour of the very best kind. They would not understand that the pressure of duties, the demands of the ministry, and the needs of North London, forced me to stop doing a job that I came to love, but they must wonder why I have stopped running along Lordship Lane!

Epilogue

Two years after I began at Tottenham Hotspur Football Club, a reporter approached me and offered a substantial sum of money if I would tell my side of the story of behind-the-scenes life at the Spurs. I refused that offer because it was obvious that it would ruin my relationship with the lads, and dash all hopes of further similar sports chaplaincies in other clubs (even though the money would have come in useful for a lowly-paid pastor). This book does not replace that 'story', because here I have sought to be on a serious mission. The reader should be able to see the difference between this and a three thousand word article in a tabloid newspaper.

A year after that offer had been made to me, I was approached by another club and asked if I would transfer (as if I was a player!). The offer was very attractive because I would have been able to insist on certain conditions and would have been given a full-time post. However, I had to refuse that offer as well, because it would have meant retiring from the work into which the Lord had called me, and from which He had not then released me.

This book is my offering to the work of sports chaplains everywhere, in exchange for the joy that this ministry has brought to me and the new friends that I have gained. It is my prayer that these pages have been of some help to a few.

Bibliography

Ardiles, Osvaldo, *My Life in Football*, Sidgewick & Jackson, London UK, 1983.
Diles, David, *Twelfth Man in the Huddle*, Word Books, USA, 1980.
Dominguez, Richard H., *Complete Book of Sports Medicine*, Warner Books, N.Y., USA, 1979.
Golesworthy, Maurice, *Encyclopaedia of Association Football*, Robert Hale, London, 1976.
Grant, Jack, *Jack Grant's Story*, Lutterworth Press, London UK, 1980.
Greaves, Jimmy, *This one's on me*, Arthur Barker, London UK, 1979.
Harris, Myron & Norman, June, *Private Life of the American Teenager*, Rawson Wade, USA, 1983.
Hoddle, Glenn, *An Autobiography*, Pelham Books, London UK, 1982.
Jennings, Pat, *An Autobiography*, Collins, London UK, 1983.
Lightbrown, Chris, *The Football Handbook*, Wolfe Publishing, London UK, 1974.
Moore, Bobby, *Soccer–the Modern Way*, Stanley Paul, London UK, 1967.
Motson, John & Rowlinson, John, *The European Cup*, Queen Anne Press, London UK, 1980.
Moynihan, John, *Park Football*, Pelham Books, London UK, 1970.
Neal, Wes, *Athletic Perfection*, Institute for Athletic Perfection, Prescott USA, 1979.
Owen, Brian, *Guide to Soccer Training*, Pelham Books, London UK, 1973.
Rous, Stanley, *Football Worlds*, Faber and Faber, London UK, 1978.
Smith, Mike, *Success in Football*, John Murray, London UK, 1978.

Stingley, Darryl, *Happy to be alive*, Beaufort Books, USA, 1983.
Swaddling, Judith, *The Ancient Olympic Games*, The British Museum, London UK, 1980.
Varney, Mike, & Harris, Harry, *Treatment of Football Injuries*, MacDonald & James, UK, 1977.
Warner, Gary, *Competition*, David C. Cook, Elgin, USA, 1979.
Williams, Gerald, *A Whole New Ball Game*, Marshall Morgan & Scott, UK, 1983.

Handbook on Hospital Chaplaincy, CIO Publishing, London, UK, 1984.
Our Ministry & Other Faiths – A Booklet for Chaplains, CIO Publishing, London, UK, 1983.
Prison Chaplain, The Home Office, Her Majesty's Stationery Office, London, UK, 1983.

Also, local and national British newspapers and national and international sports magazines.

Index